NOSH GLUTEN-FREE BAKING

by Joy May & the family team

THE NOSH SERIES OF COOKBOOKS BY JOY MAY

NEW
NOSH SUGAR-FREE GLUTEN-FREE
JOY MAY
ISBN: 9780993260919

NOSH GLUTEN-FREE BAKING
ANOTHER NO-FUSS, GLUTEN-FREE COOKBOOK FROM THE MAY FAMILY
JOY MAY
ISBN: 9780956746498

NOSH GLUTEN-FREE
JOY MAY
ISBN: 9780956746450

NOSH QUICK & EASY
JOY MAY
ISBN: 9780956746481

ISBN: 9780956746474

NOSH FOR STUDENTS VOL.2
THE SEQUEL TO 'NOSH FOR STUDENTS' ...GET THE OTHER ONE FIRST !!
OVER 200,000 STUDENT NOSH BOOKS SOLD
JOY MAY
ISBN: 9780956746467

ISBN: 9780954317973

ISBN: 9780956746443

Contents

Letter From Joy

I discovered that I was 'gluten intolerant' a couple of years ago whilst I was writing 'Nosh Gluten-Free'. Friends had asked me to write a gluten-free book, but during the process, I realised that the stomach pains, which I had thought were due to medication I was taking, were significantly relieved when I cut out gluten from my diet. I was glad to find the cause of the problem, but knew that this would make life challenging!

So I began my journey of gluten-free living with the book 'NOSH Gluten-Free' to help me and now I have added this latest book, 'NOSH Gluten-Free Baking'. I have to be frank and say that the 'Baking' book has been the hardest book I have ever written; I have never had to deal with so many failed attempts in all my years of cooking! For instance, bread depends on gluten for its elasticity and 'bounce'. I must have made about 50 different breads, all of which ended up in the bin, before coming up with the new ones in this book, and my quest still goes on to find more.

During the process of writing this book, one of the highlights would definitely be the puff pastry recipe. When that pastry came out of the oven, with its distinct, crispy layers, I could have done a little jig in the kitchen, right there and then!

When we find we are gluten intolerant, or 'coeliac', it can seem like a 'life sentence of no treats'. We go into a cafe for coffee and cake and often find there is nothing we can eat - all the 'yummy'-looking ones are full of gluten! My aim in this book has been to reverse the 'sentence'. I have tried to include recipes for the many things we might like to eat in the coffee shops, as well as the regular desserts and savoury pastries that seemed to be 'forbidden'. I hope that you enjoy cooking and eating many of these re-found treats.

Joy

Why is Eating Gluten-free on the Increase?

The most common reason for people eating a gluten-free diet is that they are either coeliac, or just have 'intolerance' to wheat. Coeliac disease is an 'auto-immune' disease affecting the gut and other parts of the body. Along with gluten intolerance, it commonly gives symptoms such as bloating, abdominal discomfort, muscular disturbances, headaches, migraines, severe fatigue and bone or joint pain. If we are gluten intolerant, when we eat gluten, it can cause the lining of our gut to become inflamed and thereby diminishes its ability to absorb certain nutrients.

But why does there seem to be a sudden emergence of people who are gluten intolerant? Dr. William Davis, in his book 'Wheat Belly", highlights our heavy dependence on wheat in the modern diet, but points out that the wheat we eat today bears little resemblance, biochemically, to the wheat which was eaten by ancient man or, indeed, that eaten by our grandparents 50 years ago. Since World War II, wheat has been heavily hybridised to increase crop yield and to increase certain baking characteristics or taste. As Dr. Davis states, "small changes in wheat protein structure can spell the difference between a devastating immune response to wheat protein, versus no immune response at all."

In addition to those who are gluten intolerant, some sports personalities, by choice, now choose gluten-free diets to improve their performance and many fitness instructors now advise cutting-out gluten completely from the diet for overall health, fitness and weight-loss reasons. Wheat is a type of 'carb' that is unique, in that it is digested so quickly that it highly affects blood sugar more than most other carb sources. Dr. Davis even states: "Aside from some extra fibre, eating two slices of whole wheat bread is really little different, and often worse, than drinking a can of sugar-sweetened soda or eating a sugary candy bar."

So, unless our wheat changes back to its original form, it would seem that there will continue to be an increasing trend towards a gluten-free diet.

When I write, I have one aim in mind: to create recipes which are easy to follow and ones that people will actually use! Some have resulted in being lengthy in order to achieve the desired result, but all are easily attainable.

In some recipes it is possible to just substitute gluten-free flour for wheat flour and add a little xanthan gum, but these are few and far between. Most need a lot more 'tweaking' than that. Gluten-free flour tends to be 'heavier' that wheat flour, and so the amount of raising-agent required varies with each recipe. Add too much raising-agent and the cake will rise to begin with, then plummet and resemble something like a 'spent volcano'. The gluten in normal wheat flours is the ingredient that gives elasticity and bounce to bread, or cakes, and holds them together. Some gluten-free bakers will recommend lots of different flours, but in this book I have, as a rule, used Doves Farm plain and self-raising flour, which usually contains a mix of rice, potato, tapioca, maize and buckwheat flour. Rice flour can also work well. Remember to use gluten-free baking powder and bicarbonate of soda. Polenta is a great ingredient in both sweet and savoury baking. I have found it to be an excellent conveyor of flavour, but do remember that there is a fine and a coarse polenta. There are one or two ingredients which, currently, are only available on the internet.

I have tested all the recipes in this book many times to make them work well, so I hope you enjoy cooking and eating them. Tim has taken some amazing photos to inspire you and we have all had a lot of fun creating this book. Our friends have been well supplied with the resulting 'goodies', as we could not manage to eat everything. They have been well received and enjoyed, so we hope you, too, will enjoy them.

Foods to Avoid and Enjoy

This section just deals with the things you would use in baking and is not an exhaustive list of all the foodstuffs you need to avoid. I find that the hidden traces of malt and barley have the worst effects; they are mainly in chocolate, sweets and cereal products.

Avoid

- wheat flours
- semolina
- spelt flour
- barley
- malted and malted chocolate
- malted milk
- rye
- bulgar wheat

Watch out for traces of gluten in the following:

- oats and cereals
- soya milk
- rice milk
- sweets and chocolate
- mustards
- ice creams
- baking powder
- bicarbonate of soda
- suet
- yeast, buy GF if you are celiac
- cherries, best to buy organic
- instant coffee, if you are especially sensitive, use fresh ground coffee

Enjoy

- gluten-free flours, plain, self-raising, bread flours, etc.
- polenta
- almond flour
- ground almonds
- rice flour
- cornflour
- GF oats
- chickpea flour (garam flour)
- GF cereals, cornflakes, puffed rice, etc.
- nuts, chopped, ground, etc.

Storecupboard

I have listed below the most frequently used ingredients in the book. Keeping them in the storecupboard means that you can always produce yourself GF goodies.

- gluten-free plain, self-raising, white bread, brown bread, flour
- rice flour
- almond flour
- cornflour
- grounds almonds
- chickpea flour
- polenta, fine and coarse
- GF oats
- GF bicarbonate of soda
- GF baking powder
- xanthan gum
- granulated sugar
- caster sugar
- icing sugar
- soft brown sugar
- dark, soft brown sugar
- golden syrup
- condensed milk
- butter
- eggs

- chocolate chips, dark, milk and white
- chocolate, dark, milk and white
- cocoa
- dessicated coconut

Nuts

- hazelnuts, ground, whole, toasted
- almonds, whole, balanced, flaked, ground
- pistachios
- pecans

Dried fruits

- apricots, raisins, currants, sultanas, cranberries

Seeds

- pumpkin, sesame, sunflower

- jams, raspberry, apricot, marmalade, honey
- vanilla bean paste
- stem ginger
- spices, cinnamon, allspice, mixed spice

Equipment

A food processor
B food mixer
C hand mixer

Even in 'normal' baking it is essential to mix and beat foods well. This applies more so in gluten-free baking. Things like 'beating butter and sugar together until light and fluffy' really requires some mechanical assistance. I would be lost without the food mixer and hand mixer.

Pastry is best if handled as little as possible and, using a food processor, I find makes great pastry and takes the hard work out of the task.

Measuring jugs
In our previous books we have used a 300ml mug as a measure, however, we decided that baking, and especially gluten-free baking, needed much more precise measurements, so have reverted to scales for this book.

D measuring spoons, etc.
E scales

Baking tins, etc. which we use in the book are as follows:
F 23 and 20cm springform tins
G 2 x 20cm shallow cake tins
H 2 x 12 hole bun tins
I 20 x 30cm tray-bake tin
J 2 flat baking sheets
K 2lb and 3lb loaf tins
L 20cm loose flan ring

Here are a few extra items that would make your life a little easier:
M zester
N sieve
O small sieve
P lemon juicer
Q baking beans
R cooling racks

D
B
Q
N
A
C
D
H
O
M
K
E
P
J
L
R
G
K
I
F
F

Shortcrust Pastry

Basic Method

1 Put the dry ingredients and butter in the food processor. Blitz until you have something resembling breadcrumbs.

2 Add the wet ingredients and pulse until you have a soft dough.

3 Turn out onto a floured sheet of cling film and roll until it is 5mm thick. Use the cling flim to help lift the pastry onto the rolling pin and transfer to the tin or dish.

Shortcrust Pastry Variations

Basic

360g **GF plain flour**

1 teaspoon **xanthan gum**

$^{1}/_{2}$ teaspoon **salt**

175g **cold butter**

1 **egg** + 75ml **cold water**

Sweet

360g **GF plain flour**

1 teaspoon **xanthan gum**

$^{1}/_{2}$ teaspoon **salt**

175g **cold butter**

100g **caster sugar**

1 **egg** + 75ml **cold water**

Chocolate

335g **GF plain flour**

2 tablespoons **cocoa**

1 teaspoon **xanthan gum**

$^{1}/_{2}$ teaspoon **salt**

100g **caster sugar**

175g **cold butter**

1 **egg** + 75ml **cold water**

Almond

100g **almond flour**

260g **GF plain flour**

1 teaspoon **xanthan gum**

175g **butter**

60g **caster sugar**

75ml **cold water**

Cheese

360g **GF plain flour**

1 teaspoon **xanthan gum**

$^{1}/_{2}$ teaspoon **salt**

1 pinch **paprika**

100g **butter**

75g grated **Cheddar cheese**

1 **egg** + 75ml **cold water**

1 beaten **egg**, to brush top with

Add the cheese just before adding the liquid.

Chickpea

150g **GF plain Flour**

150g **chickpea flour**

150g **butter**

1$^{1}/_{2}$ teaspoon **xanthan gum**

$^{1}/_{2}$ teaspoon **salt**

90ml **cold water**

Rough Puff Pastry

150g **frozen butter**
270g **GF bread flour**
1 teaspoon **xanthan gum**
150ml **cold water**
pinch **salt**

1. Grate half the frozen butter and add to the flour and xanthan gum. Mix and then gradually add enough water until the mixture forms a soft dough.

2. Turn out onto a floured sheet of cling film and roll into an oblong, approximately 30cm x 20cm.

3. Grate the other half of the butter and spread over dough. Roll the dough up like a Swiss roll, using the cling film to help.

4. Fold over the top ⅓ and then fold up the bottom ⅓. Press together, the pastry will be quite rough. Wrap in cling film and place in the fridge for 30 minutes.

5. Take out of the fridge and roll again to the 30 x 20cm oblong. Fold the top ⅓ over and the bottom ⅓ up. Press together, wrap in the cling film and put back in the fridge for 30 minutes. Repeat twice more (4 folds in all) and refrigerate for 30 minutes.

Baking Blind

Baking blind is very easy and it prevents 'soggy bottoms' . All you need to do, once you have lined the tin or flan ring with pastry, is to take a sheet of greaseproof paper which is larger than the tin, scrunch it up and unfold it and then gently put it in the pastry. Pour in some baking beans (cheap as chips in Dunhelm), or some lentils, to weigh down the paper. Bake in the oven for the specified time. Carefully remove and return the pastry to the oven for the specified time.

Lining Cake Tins

Many tins these days are already non-stick and just need to be greased lightly. Using a sunflower spray oil is fine for this purpose. If a cake is going to be in the oven for a long time, Christmas cakes for example, the cake needs a little more protection and so lining the tin helps.

Using Greaseproof Paper

Tray bake and Swiss roll tins just need an oblong of paper, larger than the tin, with diagonal cuts in each corner. Grease the tin lightly to help the paper stick.
Round cake tins need the sides lined first. Cut a long strip of paper, taller than the tin, fold over the bottom 3cm and make diagonal cuts all the way along to enable the paper to sit in the tin. Grease the tin lightly to hold the paper in place. Cut a circle of paper for the bottom.

Double Lining

To 'double line' just means to put 2 layers of greaseproof paper in the tins, greasing lightly between each. I find using a light spray oil works well for this. The reason for this is to protect the cake during long cooking times. Sometimes, when cooking cakes that need a long time in the oven, it can also be helpful to wrap a piece of foil around the outside of the tin to prevent the cake from burning, or becoming dry around the edges.

Teflon Sheets

I find these great and have many that are cut to size for various tins. They last for a good while if they are washed carefully and save lots of time cutting greaseproof paper to size each time. They are also good for lining the baking sheets for cookies, etc.

Fondant Icing

450g **icing sugar**

2 tablespoons **liquid glucose**

1 **egg white**

1 Put everything in the food processor and mix until a paste is formed. Turn out onto a surface dusted with icing sugar and knead until smooth.

2 Wrap in cling film until needed.

Marzipan

175g **caster sugar**

280g **icing sugar**

450g **ground almonds**

2 **eggs**, beaten

1 Place the marzipan ingredients in a food processor and whizz until the mixture forms a dough.

2 Turn out onto a surface dusted with icing sugar. Knead a little to be sure it is evenly mixed. Wrap in cling film until needed.

Salted Caramel

1 mug/140g **soft brown sugar**

90g **butter**

1/3 mug/100ml **double cream**

1 teaspoon **sea salt**

NOTE: Try this with ice cream, nuts or cheesecake.

1 Put the sugar, butter and cream in a small saucepan. Gently bring to the boil and simmer for 3 minutes.

2 Add the salt. Taste, but be careful as it will be hot! Use with ice cream and other desserts.

Rolling a Swiss Roll

1 Put a tea towel on a work surface. Top with a large sheet of greaseproof paper and sprinkle with caster sugar.

2 As soon as the cake is cooked, turn out onto the paper.

3 Gently remove the greaseproof paper which the cake has cooked in.

4 Roll the cake up, making sure that the greaseproof paper stays between the layers.

5 Cover with the tea towel and leave to cool.

6 Once the cake is cooled, gently unroll and fill with the jam and cream and carefully roll up again.

7 Dredge with icing sugar.

CAKES, TARTS...AND ONE WHIRL

Chocolate Fudge Cake

200g **butter**, measure using packet

200g **dark brown sugar**

4 **eggs**

3 tablespoons **golden syrup**

250g **GF self-raising flour**

1 teaspoon **xanthan gum**

1 teaspoon **GF baking powder**

50g **cocoa**

1 teaspoon **vanilla extract**

75ml **milk**

Topping

200ml **double cream**

200g **dark chocolate**

zest of an **orange**

1. Preheat the oven to 160°C fan oven/180°C/gas 5. Grease and line 2 x 20cm tins.
2. Beat together the butter and sugar until light and fluffy. Add the eggs, one at a time, beating well between each addition.
3. Add the syrup and beat well.
4. Add the flour, xanthan gum, baking powder, cocoa, vanilla and milk and gently mix together.
5. Divide between the 2 tins and smooth out the tops. Place in the oven for 25 minutes. Leave to cool.
6. Put the cream in a small saucepan and bring to the boil. Take off the heat and add the chocolate. Stir until the chocolate melts. Add the orange zest and stir. Leave to cool. When the chocolate begins to set, put a little on the base of one of the cakes and place the other one, base down, on top. Pour the rest of the chocolate over the top and spread over the cake. Leave to set; although, you can try a piece before it is set - just a bit messy, but yummy.

So you like chocolate do you? Why not try our chocolate pancakes over at noshbooks.com/chocpancake

Carrot Cake

175g **butter**, softened

100g **soft brown sugar**

zest of an **orange**

2 **eggs**

55g **GF plain flour**

1 teaspoon **xanthan gum**

1 teaspoon **GF baking powder**

2 teaspoons **mixed spice**

115g **ground almonds**

1 medium **carrot**, coarsley grated

85g **raisins**

85g **candied peel**

55g **roasted chopped hazelnuts**

Topping

25g **roasted chopped hazelnuts**

100g **icing sugar**

juice of an **orange**

1 Preheat the oven to 180°C fan oven/200°C/gas 6. Grease and line a 20cm springform cake tin.

2 Beat together the butter, sugar and orange zest until light and fluffly.

3 Add the eggs, one at a time, beating well between each addition .

4 Add the rest of the ingredients and mix gently.

5 Place in the prepared tin and smooth over the top to make the cake even.

6 Bake for 30–35 minutes. The cake should spring back lightly when gently pressed. Test with a skewer to see that the centre is cooked.

7 Mix the icing sugar with enough orange juice to make a thick paste. Once the cake is cooled, drizzle the icing over and sprinkle with the chopped hazelnuts.

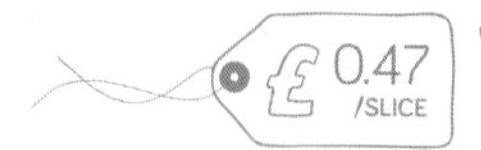

Tiramisu Cake

Some instant coffees can contain gluten, so if you are especially sensitive, use 1 tablespoon of very strong, fresh coffee, instead of the coffee and hot water.

200g **butter**
200g **caster sugar**
4 **eggs**
130g **GF self-raising flour**
1 teaspoon **GF baking powder**
1 teaspoon **xanthan gum**
80g **ground almonds**
1 tablespoon **cold water**

½ tablespoon **instant coffee**
1 tablespoon **hot water**
2 tablespoons **icing sugar**
3 tablespoons **white rum**

125g **mascarpone cheese**
200ml **double cream**
½ teaspoon **vanilla bean paste**
1 tablespoon **icing sugar**
50g **milk chocolate**, grated
cocoa

1. Preheat the oven to 180°C fan oven/200°C/gas 6. Grease and line 2 x 22cm cake tins.
2. Beat together the butter and sugar until light and fluffly.
3. Add the eggs, one at a time, beating well between each addition.
4. Add the flour, baking powder, xanthan gum, ground almonds and cold water. Fold in gently.
5. Divide between the two tins. Smooth out evenly. Bake in the oven for 25 minutes.
6. Mix together the coffee, hot water and icing sugar until the coffee has dissolved, then add the rum.
7. Once the cakes are cooled, brush the coffee mix over the top of each cake and allow to soak in.
8. Beat together the mascarpone, cream, vanilla and icing sugar until it thickens.
9. Put about ⅓ of the cream mixture on top of one of the cakes. Sandwich the other cake on top and put the rest of the cream mixture on top.
10. Top with grated chocolate and dredge over some cocoa.

Pear and Raspberry Cake

185g softened **butter**

275g **caster sugar**

6 **eggs**

125g **GF self-raising flour**

$\frac{1}{2}$ teaspoon **xanthan gum**

2 teaspoons **ground cinnamon**

400g **ground almonds**

2 **fresh pears**, peeled and sliced

100g **fresh raspberries**

1 tablespoon **soft brown sugar**

1. Preheat the oven to 150°C fan oven/170°C/gas 4. Grease and line a 23cm cake tin.
2. Beat together the butter and sugar.
3. Add the eggs, one at a time, beating well between each addition.
4. Gently fold in the flour, xanthan gum, cinnamon and almonds.
5. Spread evenly in the cake tin. Arrange the fruit on the top, see photo. Sprinkle the tablespoon of soft brown sugar over the top.
6. Bake in the oven for $1\frac{1}{2}$ hours.

 We have got another cake for you to try over at noshbooks.com/limecake

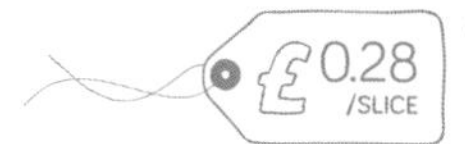

Orange Pistachio Cake

150g **butter**

150g **granulated sugar**

2 **eggs**

50g **ground almonds**

150g **pistachio**, roughly chopped

rind and juice of an **orange**

150g **GF self-raising flour**

1 teaspoon **GF baking powder**

1 teaspoon **xanthan gum**

3 tablespoons good quality **orange marmalade**

2 tablespoons **icing sugar**

1. Preheat the oven to 160°C fan oven/180°C/gas 5. Grease and line a 20cm cake tin.
2. Beat together the butter and sugar until light and fluffy. Add the eggs, one at a time, beating well between each addition.
3. Add the almonds, pistachios, orange, flour, baking powder and xanthan gum and fold in gently. Spoon into the cake tin. Smooth out until even.
4. Place in the oven for 45 minutes.
5. Take out of the oven and spread over the marmalade. Mix the icing sugar with a small amount of water and drizzle over the top. Leave to cool in the tin.

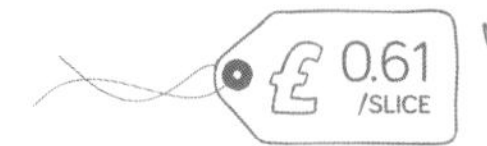

Chocolate Orange Polenta Cake

100g **dark chocolate**
200g **butter**
200g **caster sugar**
3 **eggs**
zest of an **orange**
200g **ground almonds**
120g **fine polenta**
2 tablespoons **cocoa**

4 tablespoons **orange marmalade**

juice of an **orange**
4 tablespoons **granulated sugar**

1. Preheat the oven to 160°C fan oven/180°C/gas 5. Grease and line 2 x 20cm cake tins.
2. Melt the chocolate in a bowl over gently simmering water. Leave to cool a little.
3. Beat together the butter and sugar. Add the eggs, one at a time, beating well between each addition.
4. Add the melted chocolate and beat well.
5. Add the orange zest, almonds, polenta and cocoa and gently fold in.
6. Divide the mixture between the two cake tins and smooth out. Place in the oven for 40 minutes.
7. Once cooked, leave to cool a little. Sandwich the cakes together with the marmalade. Mix together the orange juice and sugar and spoon over the top cake.
8. Leave to cool and then serve.

 Loving polenta right now? For more, head over to noshbooks.com/lemonpolenta

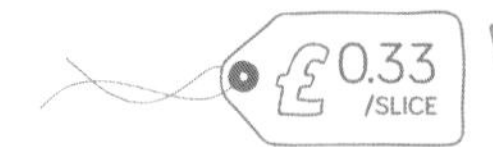

Mocha Ring

Looks pretty impressive. It is so easy to bake and the decoration just requires a lack of inhibition, in order to flick the melted chocolate back and forth. Do wear an apron though! Some instant coffee can contain gluten, so use 2 tablespoons of very strong, freshly brewed coffee in place of the coffee and water.

3 tablespoons **instant coffee granules**

$2\frac{1}{2}$ tablespoons **cocoa**

150ml **buttermilk**

2 tablespoons **water**

300g **butter**, measure using packet

300g **caster sugar**

6 **eggs**

100g **ground almonds**

200g **rice flour**

2 teaspoons **GF baking powder**

1 teaspoon **xanthan gum**

Topping

250g **icing sugar**

80g **butter**, measure using packet

2 tablespoons **soured cream**

2 tablespoons **cocoa**

75g **dark chocolate**

1. Preheat the oven to 170°C fan oven/190°C/gas 5. Grease 23cm cake ring.
2. Mix together the coffee, cocoa, buttermilk and water in a small bowl.
3. Beat together the butter and sugar until light and fluffy. Add the eggs, one at a time, beating well between each addition.
4. Add the coffee and beat well.
5. Add the almonds, rice flour, baking powder and xanthan gum and gently mix together. Spoon into the cake ring and spread evenly.
6. Bake in the oven for 40 minutes. Turn the oven down to 150°C fan oven/170°C/gas 4 and bake for a further 10 minutes.
7. Turn out of the tin and leave to cool.
8. Beat together the icing sugar, butter, soured cream and cocoa. Spread over the cake.
9. Melt the dark chocolate in a bowl over a pan of simmering water. Once melted, drizzle over the cake. Leave to set.

Buttermilk Sponge with 'Philly' Filling

The buttermilk makes this sponge delightfully light for a gluten-free cake. One of the lightest I have made.

120g **butter**

300g **caster sugar**

2 **eggs**

2 teaspoons **vanilla bean paste**

240ml **buttermilk**

4 tablespoons **cold water**

3 teaspoons **white wine vinegar**

300g **rice flour**

1 teaspoon **xanthan gum**

1 teaspoon **GF bicarbonate of soda**

Icing

250g **icing sugar**

50g **butter**

125g **Philadelphia cream cheese**

1. Preheat the oven to 150°C fan oven/170°C/gas 4. Prepare 2 x 20cm cake tins.
2. Beat together the butter and sugar. Add the eggs, one at a time, beating well between each addition. Add the vanilla and beat well.
3. In a separate bowl, mix together the buttermilk, water and vinegar.
4. Sift together the flour, xanthan gum and bicarbonate of soda. Add half to the bowl along with half the buttermilk mix and gently fold in. Add the other half of the flour and buttermilk and fold in. Divide between the two cake tins and smooth over evenly. Place in the oven for 40 minutes.
5. Leave to cool.
6. Beat together the icing ingredients and spread over one of the cakes. Spread the jam over the other one and sandwich together.

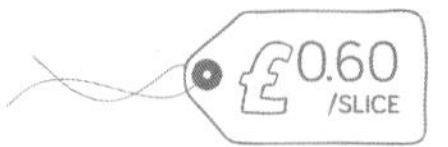

Battenberg

150g **butter**
150g **caster sugar**
3 **eggs**
100g **self-raising flour**
100g **ground almonds**
1 teaspoon **GF baking powder**
1 teaspoon **xanthan gum**
1 teaspoon **almond extract**
red food colouring

apricot jam

1 quantity of **marzipan**, see page 16

1. Preheat the oven to 160°C fan oven/180°C/gas 5. Grease and line 2 loaf tins.
2. Beat together the butter and sugar and add the eggs, one at a time, beating well between each addition.
3. Add the flour, almonds, baking powder, xanthan gum, and almond extract.
4. Put half the mixture in the bottom of one of the loaf tins and spread evenly.
5. Add a small amount of red food colouring to the remaining mixture and gently mix. Place in the other loaf tin and spread out evenly.
6. Bake in the oven for 25 minutes. Leave to cool.
7. Cut each cake in half, lengthways, and trim to make even quarters for the cake. Arrange into the classic Battenberg formation, brushing the warmed apricot jam between each surface.
8. On a sheet of cling flim, dusted with icing sugar, roll out the marzipan until it is 3mm thick. Brush one side of the cake with the apricot jam and place on the marzipan. Brush the next side and roll onto the marzipan. Continue until all sides are covered with the marzipan. Trim off the excess marzipan and tidy up the ends by taking a small slice off each end.
9. Eat the ends you have just trimmed off. You deserve it!

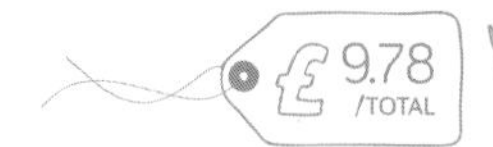

Christmas Cake

150g **currants**
150g **sultanas**
150g **raisins**
100g **glace cherries**, halved
50g **mixed peel**
zest and juice of a **lemon**
150ml **port**, **sherry** or **brandy**
175g softened **butter**
175g **soft brown sugar**
3 **eggs**
100g **GF self-raising flour**
2 teaspoons **xanthan gum**
1 teaspoon **cinnamon**
½ teaspoon **nutmeg**
1 teaspoon **ginger**
1 teaspoon **allspice**
85g ground **almonds**

½ quantity **marzipan**, see page 16
2 x **fondant icing recipe**, see page 16

1. Preheat the oven to 150°C fan oven/170°C/gas 4. Grease and double line a 20cm cake tin.
2. Put the currants, sultanas, raisins, cherries, peel, lemon zest and juice and port in a large bowl. Mix together and leave for 2 hours to soak.
3. Beat together the butter and the sugar. Add the eggs, one at a time, beating in between each addition.
4. Add the flour, xantham gum, cinnamon, nutmeg, ginger, allspice and ground almonds. Mix well.
5. Add the fruits and mix well.
6. Pour into the cake tin and bake in the oven for 2 hours, checking after 1 hour. If the cake is browning on the top too quickly, put a piece of greaseproof, or brown paper, over the top to prevent further browning. Check that the cake is cooked by inserting a skewer. If it comes out clean, then it is cooked.
7. Ideally, leave for a few days.
8. To decorate, roll out the marzipan and mould over the cake. Decorate using 1 quantity of fondant icing to cover the whole cake and another quantity, mixed with various food colourings, if you want to decorate like the photo opposite.

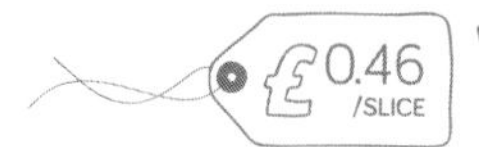

Panforte

This is an Italian Christmas cake which originates in Sienna. It should keep for up to six months in a tin. I was unable to prove that fact!

150g **hazelnuts**
150g **whole blanched almonds**
125g **candied peel**
100g **candied pineapple**, chopped
75g **GF plain flour**
zest of a **lemon**
½ teaspoon **xanthan gum**
1 teaspoon **ground cinnamon**
¼ teaspoon **ground coriander**
¼ teaspoon **ground cloves**
¼ teaspoon **ground nutmeg**
150g **caster sugar**
4 tablespoons **honey**
50g **butter**
icing to dust

1. Preheat the oven to 130°C fan oven/150°C/gas 3. Grease and line a 20cm springform tin.
2. Place the hazelnuts and almonds in a dry frying pan and toast until lightly browned. Keep them moving in the pan to prevent burning.
3. Put the nuts in a large bowl together with the peel, pineapple, flour, lemon, xanthan gum and spices.
4. Put the sugar, honey and butter in a small saucepan and gently bring to the boil. Simmer gently for 5 minutes.
5. Pour into the bowl and mix everything together.
6. Transfer to the cake tin and spread out evenly.
7. Bake for 35 minutes.
8. Once cool, take out of the tin and dredge with icing sugar. Cut into small pieces.

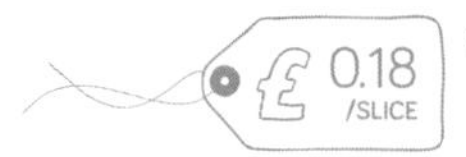

Swiss Roll

3 **eggs**, separated

100g **caster sugar**

zest of a **lemon**

40g **rice flour**

40g **cornflour**

½ teaspoon **GF baking powder**

4 tablespoons **raspberry jam**

200ml **double cream**, whipped

1. Preheat the oven to 160°C fan oven/180°C/gas 5. You will need a 23 x 33cm Swiss roll tin. Line the tin with greaseproof paper and very lightly grease the top side of the paper.
2. Beat the eggs yolks and half the caster sugar until pale in colour. Add the lemon zest.
3. Beat the egg whites until stiff and slowly add the other half of the sugar, whilst still beating. The mixture should be stiff and shiny.
4. In a separate bowl, sift together the rice flour, cornflour and baking powder.
5. Gently fold everything together, trying not to lose the air from the egg whites.
6. Pour into the prepared tin and spread out to level.
7. Bake in the oven for 15 minutes.
8. Put a tea towel on a work surface, with a large sheet of greaseproof paper on top. Sprinkle with caster sugar. As soon as the cake is cooked, turn out onto the paper. Gently remove the greaseproof paper that the cake has cooked in and roll the cake up, making sure that the greaseproof paper stays between the layers. Cover with the tea towel and leave to cool. For more tips on how to do this, see page 17.
9. Once the cake is cooled, unroll and spread with the jam and then the cream. Re-roll and dredge with icing sugar.

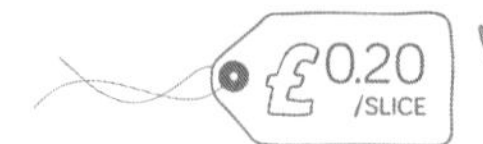

Bara Brith

175g **currants**
175g **sultanas**
225g **soft brown sugar**
300ml **strong black tea**
1 large **egg**, beaten
275g **GF self-raising flour**
1 teaspoon **xanthan gum**
½ teaspoon **GF baking powder**

1. Put the currants, sultanas and sugar in a large bowl and pour over the hot tea. Leave to stand for at least an hour, preferably overnight.
2. Preheat the oven to 150°C fan oven/170°C/gas 3. You will need a greased 2lb loaf tin.
3. Add the beaten egg to the fruit mix, add the dry ingredients and gently mix until smooth.
4. Pour into the loaf tin. Bake in the oven for 1½ hours. The cake should have risen and be firm to the touch.
5. Leave to cool before spreading with butter.

V

Lemon Ginger Cupcakes

200g **butter**

200g **caster sugar**

4 **eggs**

130g **GF self-raising flour**

1 teaspoon **GF baking powder**

1 teaspoon **xanthan gum**

80g **ground almonds**

1 tablespoon cold **water**

120g **stem ginger**, chopped

Icing

25ml **milk**

300g **icing sugar**

100g **butter**

zest of a **lemon**

crystallised ginger to decorate

NOTE: I have used crystallised ginger to decorate the tops of the cakes, but you can use stem ginger if you wish.

1. Preheat the oven to 160°C fan oven/180°C/gas 5. You will need a 12 hole bun tin filled with muffin cases.
2. Beat together the butter and sugar until light and fluffy.
3. Add the eggs, one at a time, beating well between each addition.
4. Add the rest of the cake ingredients and gently fold in until smooth.
5. Bake in the oven for 25 minutes. The cakes will be nicely golden brown and spring back when lightly pressed.
6. Leave to cool and make the icing. Put the milk, icing sugar, butter and lemon zest in the mixer and beat well until smooth.
7. Spread over the cooled cakes and sprinkle over with the chopped ginger.

Blueberry Muffins

360g **GF self-raising flour**

1 teaspoon **GF baking powder**

1 teaspoon **xanthan gum**

360g **caster sugar**

½ teaspoon **GF bicarbonate of soda**

250g **fresh blueberries**

375ml **buttermilk**

1 **egg**

1 teaspoon **vanilla extract**

70g **butter**, melted

1. Preheat the oven to 170°C fan oven/190°C/gas 5. Prepare 15 muffin cases.
2. Put all the dry ingredients in a large bowl and mix. Add the blueberries and mix.
3. Beat together the buttermilk, egg, vanilla and melted butter. Add to the dry ingredients and mix.
4. Spoon 2 heaped dessertspoons of the mixture into each muffin case.
5. Bake in the oven for 35–40 minutes. The muffins should be lightly browned and spring back when gently pressed.

Butterfly Cakes

120g **butter**

300g **caster sugar**

2 **eggs**

240ml **buttermilk**

4 tablespoons **cold water**

2 teaspoons **vanilla bean paste**

3 teaspoons **white wine vinegar**

300g **rice flour**

1 teaspoon **xanthan gum**

1 teaspoon **GF bicarbonate of soda**

Icing

250g **icing sugar**

150g **butter**

125g **Philadelphia cream cheese**

1. Preheat the oven to 180°C fan oven/200°C/gas 6. Prepare 2 cake tins.
2. Beat together the butter and sugar. Add the eggs, one at a time, beating well between each addition.
3. Mix together the buttermilk, water, vanilla and vinegar.
4. Sift together the flour, xanthan gum and bicarbonate of soda. Add half to the bowl, along with half the buttermilk mix and gently fold in. Fold in the other half of the flour and buttermilk. Put a heaped dessertspoon of the mixture in each cake case.
5. Place in the oven for 20 minutes and leave to cool.
6. Beat the icing ingredients together. Horizontally, cut circles out of the top of each cake and add a teaspoon of the icing mixture into the hollow. Cut the circles in half to form the wings and place on top. Dredge with icing sugar.

Chocolate Raspberry Muffins

300g **GF self-raising flour**

2 tablespoons **cocoa**

1 teaspoon **GF baking powder**

1 teaspoon **xanthan gum**

175g **soft brown sugar**

100g **white chocolate chips**

200g **frozen raspberries,** defrosted

2 **eggs**

100g **butter,** melted

200ml **milk**

1 Preheat the oven to 180°C fan oven/200°C/gas 6. Prepare 24 cases in 2 muffin trays.

2 Mix the dry ingredients together in a large bowl. Add the raspberries and gently mix.

3 Beat the eggs in a large jug, or bowl, and add the rest of the wet ingredients. Mix together and add to the dry ingredients. Mix gently.

4 Put tablespoons of the mixture in each of the cake cases.

5 Bake in the oven for 25 minutes.

6 If you use the large muffin cases, the mixture will make about 15 and you will need to cook them for 30–35 minutes.

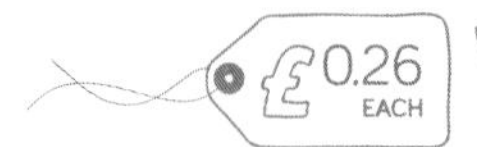

Banana Cinnamon Muffins

300g **GF self-raising flour**

1 teaspoon **GF baking powder**

1 teaspoon **xanthan gum**

½ teaspoon **GF bicarbonate of soda**

2 teaspoons **cinnamon**

175g **soft brown sugar**

100g **white chocolate chips**

50g roasted **chopped hazelnuts**

2 **eggs**, beaten

100g **butter**, melted

200ml **milk**

3 **bananas**, lightly mashed

NOTE: If you use normal cake cases, the mixture will make 18 cakes and will need to be cooked for only 25–30 minutes.

1. Preheat the oven to 180°C fan oven/200°C/gas 6. Prepare 12 muffin cases in a muffin tray.
2. Put all the dry ingredients in a large bowl.
3. In a separate bowl, mix together the eggs, melted butter and milk. Add to the ingredients, along with the mashed bananas, and mix together.
4. Spoon 2 heaped dessertspoons into each muffin case.
5. Bake in the oven for 35–40 minutes. The muffins should spring back when lightly pressed and be golden brown.

Red Velvet Cupcakes

You can use the Dr. Oetker's food colouring and the cake will be quite red, but if for some special occasion you want to make them really red, try 1 teaspoon of Wilton red gel colouring.

60g **butter**

150g **caster sugar**

1 **egg**

2 tablespoons **cocoa**

10g **Dr. Oetker's red food colouring**

1/2 teaspoon **vanilla extract**

2 tablespoons cold **water**

150g **rice flour**

1/2 teaspoon **xanthan gum**

1/2 teaspoon **GF bicarbonate of soda**

120ml **buttermilk**

1 1/2 teaspoons **white wine vinegar**

Icing

200g **icing sugar**

30g **butter**

90g **Philadelphia cream cheese**

1. Preheat the oven to 150°C fan oven/170°C/gas 4. Prepare 12 bun cases in muffin trays.
2. Beat together the butter and sugar. Add the egg and beat well.
3. Put the cocoa, food colouring, vanilla and water in a small bowl and mix to a paste. Add to the bowl and beat well.
4. Sift together the flour, xanthan gum and bicarbonate of soda. Add half to the butter and sugar mix, along with half the buttermilk, and gently fold in. Add the other half of the flour and buttermilk and fold in. Add the vinegar and gently mix in.
5. Put a heaped dessertspoon of the mixture in each cake case.
6. Bake in the oven for 25 minutes.
7. Leave to cool.
8. Beat together the icing ingredients and spread over the tops of the cup cakes.

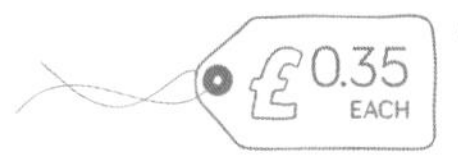

Chocolate Hazelnut Cupcakes

120g **butter**

300g **caster sugar**

2 **eggs**

240ml **buttermilk**

3 tablespoons **white wine vinegar**

80g **ground toasted hazelnuts**

150g **GF plain flour**

½ teaspoon **GF baking powder**

2 tablespoons **cocoa**

1 teaspoon **xanthan gum**

1 teaspoon **GF bicarbonate of soda**

1 tablespoon **water**

Topping

150g **butter**

250g **icing sugar**

1 tablespoon **cocoa**

2 tablespoons **milk**

25g **roasted chopped hazelnuts**

1. Preheat the oven to 180°C fan oven/200°C/gas 6. You will need 2 x 12 hole bun tins, filled with 15 muffin cases.
2. Beat together the butter and sugar until light and fluffy.
3. Add the eggs, one at a time, beating well between each addition.
4. Mix the buttermilk and vinegar together in a separate bowl. Separately, mix the dry ingredients together.
5. Add both to the butter and egg mix and gently fold in until smooth.
6. Put a heaped dessertspoon of the mixture in each muffin case.
7. Bake in the oven for 25 minutes.
8. To make the topping, put the butter, icing sugar, cocoa and milk in the mixer and beat well until it forms a yummy chocolate cream.
9. Once the cakes are cool, spread over the top of each cake and sprinkle with the hazelnuts.

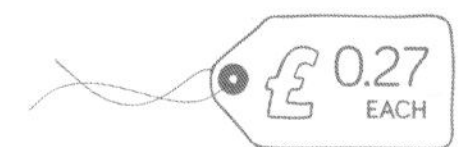

Fruit Scones

I have used almond flour here. You can use 400g GF self-raising flour, but the almond flour does give a lovely texture and flavour.

300g **GF self-raising flour**
100g **almond flour**
1 teaspoon **xanthan gum**
1 teaspoon **GF baking powder**
140g **butter**
50g **mixed fruit**
90g **sugar**
1 **egg**, made up to 200ml with milk
egg to brush
sugar to sprinkle on top

1. Preheat the oven to 180°C fan oven/200°C/gas 6. Grease and line a baking tray.
2. Put the flour, almond flour, xanthan gum, baking powder and butter in a food processor and whizz until the mixture resembles breadcrumbs.
3. Add the fruit and sugar and pulse a couple of times.
4. Add the egg and milk and pulse a few times until the dough holds together.
5. Turn the dough out onto a floured surface and squash down until aprroximately 5cm thick. Cut into rounds. Place on a baking tray. Brush the tops with the beaten egg and then sprinkle with sugar.
6. Bake in the oven for 20 minutes.

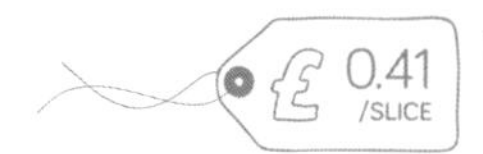

V

Simnel Slice

½ quantity of **basic shortcrust pastry**, see page 11

½ quantity **marzipan**, see page 16

Filling

150g **butter**, softened

150g **caster sugar**

3 **eggs**

100g **GF self-raising flour**

½ teaspoon **GF baking powder**

1 teaspoon **xanthan gum**

1 teaspoon **mixed spice**

1 teaspoon **ground cinnamon**

60g **ground almonds**

175g **mixed dried fruit**

50g **cherries**, halved

zest and juice of an **orange**

toasted **flaked almonds**

icing sugar

1. Preheat the oven to 180°C fan oven/200°C/gas 6. Prepare a 22cm flan ring.
2. Roll the pastry onto a sheet of floured cling film.
3. Gently fit into the tin, leaving the pastry over the edges to allow for shrinkage. Bake blind for 15 minutes, see page 14.
4. Roll out half the marzipan until it is 5mm thick. Cut into a circle just smaller than the flan tin.
5. Beat together the butter and sugar and add the eggs, one at a time, beating well between each addition.
6. Add the flour, baking powder, xanthan gum, spice, cinnamon, almonds, fruit, cherries and orange zest and juice. Fold in gently.
7. Once the pastry has been baked blind, remove from the oven and remove the baking beans, etc.
8. Put half the mixture into the tin and smooth out evenly. Place the marzipan over the mixture. Put the rest of the mixture into the tin and spread out evenly.
9. Bake in the oven for 30 minutes.
10. Meanwhile, roll the rest of the marzipan into small balls. Place on a baking tray and place under the grill until they brown lightly.
11. Drizzle the icing over and sprinkle with the almonds. Stick the little balls on with icing sugar.

Mince Pies

Mincemeat is usually made with suet which can often contain gluten. Here is a gluten-free recipe, easy to make and very delicious.

Mincemeat

1 medium **cooking apple**, peeled and cut into 1cm chunks

150ml **water**

130g **currants**

130g **sultanas**

130g **raisins**

2 tablespoons **ginger wine** or **sherry**

80g **dark brown sugar**

½ teaspoon **cinnamon**

½ teaspoon **nutmeg**

1 teaspoon **allspice**

1 quantity of **sweet shortcrust pastry**, see page 11

½ quantity of **marzipan**, see page 16

icing sugar to dust

1. To make the mincemeat, place the apples in a large pan with the water and simmer gently until the apple starts to get fluffy around the edges. Add the rest of the mincemeat ingredients and simmer for 5 minutes, stirring every now and then. Leave to cool completely before using.
2. Preheat the oven to 180°C fan oven/200°C/gas 6.
3. Make the pastry, see page 11.
4. Roll out on a sheet of floured cling film and cut 12 x 8cm diameter circles. Place in the bottom of the bun tins, fill with mincemeat.
5. Roll out the marzipan and cut out hearts or stars. Place on the tops of the pies.
6. Bake in the oven for 20 minutes.
7. Dust with a little icing sugar.

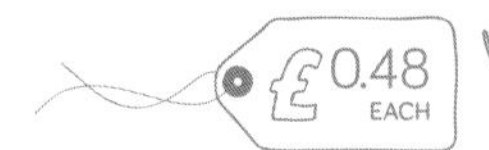

Cherry Bakewells

1 quantity of **basic shortcrust pastry**, see page 11

raspberry jam

150g softened **butter**
150g **caster sugar**
3 **eggs**
100g **GF self-raising flour**
½ teaspoon **GF baking powder**
1 teaspoon **xanthan gum**
60g ground **almonds**
1 tablespoon cold **water**

250g **icing sugar**
15 **cherries**

1. Preheat the oven to 180°C fan oven/200°C/gas 6.
2. Make the pastry and turn out onto a floured sheet of cling flim. Roll out to approximately 5mm thickness. Cut out 9cm diameter rings. Gently ease into patty tins. Put a teaspoon of raspberry jam in the bottom of each. Leave in the fridge if you have room.
3. Beat together the butter and sugar. Add the eggs, one at a time, beating well between each addition.
4. Sift together the flour, baking powder and xanthan gum. Fold into the mixture along with the almonds and water.
5. Put a heaped dessertspoon of the mixture in each of the pastry cases.
6. Bake in the oven for 25 minutes. Leave to cool.
7. Mix the icing sugar with water to form a very thick paste. Put a teaspoonful on each Bakewell and a cherry on the top.

Poppy Seed Slice

1 quantity of **basic shortcrust pastry**, see page 11

½ jar **marmalade**

Filling

150g softened **butter**
150g **caster sugar**
3 **eggs**
100g **GF self-raising flour**
1 teaspoon **xanthan gum**
60g **ground almonds**
1 tablespoon cold **water**
zest of **lemon**
30g **poppy seeds**

1 mug **icing sugar**

1. Preheat the oven to 180°C fan oven/200°C/gas 6.
2. Make the pastry, see page 11, and use it to line a 22cm flan ring or 34cm x 13cm long flan tin.
3. Spread the marmalade over the base.
4. Beat together the butter and sugar until light and fluffy.
5. Add the eggs, one at a time, beating well between each addition.
6. Add the rest of the filling ingredients and gently mix.
7. Spread evenly over the jam. Bake in the oven for 30 minutes.
8. Mix the icing sugar with sufficient water to make a stiff paste and place in an icing bag.
9. Once the cake is cooled, drizzle over the icing.

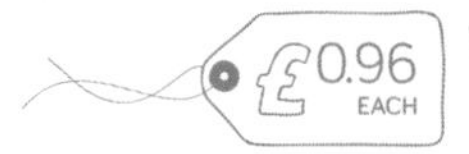

V

Berry Frangipane Tarts

1 quantity of **sweet pastry**, see page 11

Frangipane

180g **butter**

180g **caster sugar**

1 teaspoon **vanilla bean paste**

4 **eggs**

180g **ground almonds**

fruits of the forest, defrosted and drained

1. Preheat the oven to 180°C fan oven/200°C/gas 6. You will need 6 x 12cm individual tart tins, or a 12 hole bun tin.
2. Make the pastry and roll out on a floured sheet of cling flim. Cut 12 x 9cm circles and put in the small flan tins. Bake blind for 10 minutes, see page 14.
3. Turn the oven down to 160°C fan oven/180°C/gas 4.
4. To make the frangipane, beat the butter and sugar together until light and fluffy. Add the eggs, one at a time, beating well between each addition.
5. Add the vanilla bean paste and mix. Add the almonds and gently mix until smooth.
6. Divide between the flan cases.
7. Press a few fruits into the top of the frangipane.
8. Place in the oven for 30–35 minutes.

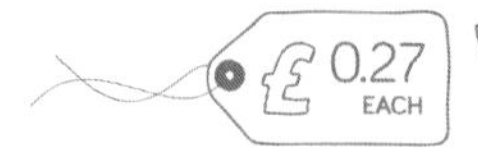

Chocolate Mousse Tarts

1 quantity of **chocolate pastry**, see page 11

Caramel

100g **soft brown sugar**
60g **butter**
75ml **double cream**

Mousse

100g **dark chocolate**
2 **eggs**, separated
30g **caster sugar**
100ml **double cream**

chocolate for the topping

1. Preheat the oven to 180°C fan oven/200°C/gas 6. You will need a 12 hole bun tin.
2. Firstly, prepare the caramel by putting the ingredients in a small pan and gently bring to the boil. Simmer for 2 minutes, take off the heat and allow to cool.
3. Make the pastry and roll out on a floured sheet of cling flim. It needs to be approx 7mm thick. Cut 12 x 9cm circles and put in the cake tin cups. Bake for 20 minutes.
4. Once the pastry is cooled, place a dessertspoon of the caramel in the bottom of each pastry tart.
5. To make the mousse, melt the chocolate in a bowl over a pan of simmering water.
6. Beat together the egg yolks and sugar until they are pale in colour. Whisk the egg whites in a separate bowl. Beat the cream in a separate bowl.
7. Add the chocolate to the egg yolks and gently mix. Add the egg whites and cream and gently fold in. Spoon into the tarts.
8. Put some shavings of chocolate on the top of each one. Keep in the fridge to set for an hour.

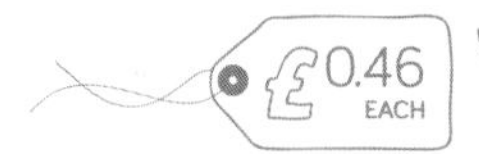

V

Frangipane and Salted Caramel Tarts

1 quantity of **sweet shortcrust pastry**, see page 11

1 quantity of **salted caramel**, see page 16

Frangipane

170g **butter**

170g **caster sugar**

3 **eggs**

1 teaspoon **vanilla bean paste**

170g **ground almonds**

24 **pecans**

1. Preheat the oven to 180°C fan oven/200°C/gas 6. You will need a 12 hole bun tin.
2. Make the caramel, see page 16.
3. Make the pastry and roll out onto a floured sheet of cling flim. The pastry should be approximately 7mm thick. Cut 12 x 9cm circles and put in the cake tin cups.
4. To make the frangipane, beat the butter and sugar together until light and fluffy. Add the eggs one at a time, beating well between each addition. Add the vanilla bean paste and almonds and mix.
5. Place a dessertspoon of the caramel in the bottom of each pastry cup. Add a heaped dessertspoon of the frangipane on top and then place 2 pecans on each tart.
6. Place in the oven for 25 minutes.

Orange and Almond Whirls

1 quantity of **rough puff pastry**, see page 12

4 tablespoons **marmalade**

4 tablespoons toasted **flaked almonds**

1 **egg**, beaten to glaze

1. Preheat the oven to 200°C fan oven/240°C/gas 9. Grease and line a baking tray.
2. Roll out the pastry onto a sheet of floured cling film until it is about 3mm thick.
3. Spread the marmalade over evenly and then sprinkle over the almonds.
4. Use the cling film to help you roll up the pastry, like a Swiss roll. Discard the cling film.
5. Using a sharp knife, cut into about 12 pieces and place each on the baking tray.
6. Brush with some beaten egg and place in the oven for 20 minutes.

COOKIES

Crackled Chocolate Cookies

100g **dark chocolate**

100g **butter**, measure using packet

150g **soft light brown sugar**

1 **egg**

160g **GF self-raising flour**

1 teaspoon **GF baking powder**

1 teaspoon **xanthan gum**

100g **white chocolate chips**

3 tablespoons **icing sugar**

1. Melt the chocolate in a bowl over a pan of simmering water. Take off the heat, add the butter and stir until it melts.
2. Add the sugar and beat well. Add the egg and beat well.
3. Add the flour, baking powder, xanthan gum and chocolate chips and gently mix together. Place in the fridge for 45 minutes.
4. Preheat the oven to 180°C fan oven/200°C/gas 6. Grease 2 large baking sheets.
5. Put the icing sugar on a plate. Take dessertspoonfuls of the cookie mixture and roll into balls; it should make about 24. Squash the balls into the icing sugar and get as much of the sugar as you can on each cookie.
6. Squash down each cookie on the baking sheets. Bake in the oven for 10–12 minutes. The cookies will be crisp on the outside and a little 'fudgy' on the inside.

Like these cookies? Why not try some apricot cookies at noshbooks.com/apricotcookies

Nutella Cookies

100g **butter**

260g **soft brown sugar**

½ x 375g pot **Nutella**

1 teaspoon **vanilla extract**

1 **egg** + 1 **egg white**

180g **GF self-raising flour**

1 teaspoon **xanthan gum**

1 tablespoon **cocoa**

50g **pecans**, roughly chopped

100g **white chocolate**

1. Preheat the oven to 180°C fan oven/200°C/gas 6. Grease 2 baking trays.
2. Beat together the butter and sugar. Add the Nutella and vanilla and beat well.
3. Add the egg and egg white and beat well.
4. Add all the dry ingredients, except the white chocolate, and gently fold in.
5. Spoon out dessertspoons of the mix and put on the baking trays. Place them well apart to give them space to spread.
6. Bake in the oven for 15 minutes.
7. Meanwhile, melt the white chocolate in a bowl over a pan of gently simmering water. Drizzle the chocolate over the cookies, see photo.

Double Chocolate Digestives

125g softened **butter**, measure using packet

180g **soft brown sugar**

1 **egg**

1 teaspoon **vanilla extract**

180g **GF self-raising flour**

2 tablespoons **cocoa**

1 teaspoon **xanthan gum**

200g **milk chocolate**

1. Beat together the butter and sugar. Add the egg and beat well.
2. Add the vanilla and beat.
3. Add the flour, cocoa and xanthan gum. Fold in until mixed thoroughly.
4. Turn the mixture out onto a sheet of cling film and form a 'sausage', approximately 6cm diameter and 25cm long. Place in the fridge for 30 minutes.
5. Preheat the oven to 180°C fan oven/200°C/gas 6. Grease 2 baking trays.
6. Cut the sausage into 12 pieces and place on the baking tray.
7. Bake in the oven for 12–14 minutes. The cookies will be crisp on the outside and a little gooey in the middle. Leave to cool.
8. Meanwhile, melt the chocolate in a pan over a pan of gently simmering water. Leave to cool until it is just beginning to set. Put a good dollop on each cookie. Using the end of a spoon, drag it through the chocolate horizontally and vertically to get the feathered effect seen on the photo.

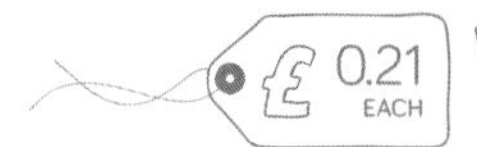

Mini Lemon Cookies

200g **butter**, measure using packet

135g **granulated sugar**

1 **egg** + 1 **egg** white

2 teaspoons **vanilla**

zest of a **lemon**

270g **GF self-raising flour**

2 teaspoons **xanthan gum**

200g **icing sugar**

juice of a **lemon**

sprinkles

1. Preheat the oven to 180°C fan oven/200°C/gas 6. Grease 2 baking trays.
2. Beat together the butter and sugar. Add the egg and egg white and beat well. Add the vanilla and lemon zest and beat.
3. Add the flour and xanthan gum and fold in gently. Tip the mixture onto a floured surface. Roll into 20 balls. Place each one on the baking trays and squash down a little.
4. Place in the oven for 14 minutes.
5. Put the icing sugar in a small bowl and add enough lemon juice to make a very stiff paste. Put a teaspoon on the top of each cookies and top with some sprinkles.

Chocolate and Peanut Butter Cookies

150g **butter**, measure using packet

190g **soft dark brown sugar**

4 tablespoons **peanut butter**

1 **egg**

100g **choc chips**

200g **GF self-raising flour**

2 tablespoons **cocoa**

1 teaspoon **xanthan gum**

50g chopped **hazelnuts**

2 tablespoons **roasted chopped hazelnuts**, for decoration

1. Preheat the oven to 180°C fan oven/200°C/gas 6. Grease 2 flat baking trays.
2. Beat together the butter and sugar. Add the peanut butter and beat again.
3. Add the egg and beat well.
4. Add the choc chips, flour, cocoa, xanthan gum and 1/2 mug hazelnuts. Gently fold in.
5. Place in a bowl in the fridge for 30 minutes.
6. Remove from the fridge and take dessertspoons of the mixture and roll into balls. Place on the trays and sqash down with a fork. Sprinkle over the 2 tablespoons of hazelnuts.
7. Bake in the oven for 14 minutes. They should be crispy on the outside and chewy in the middle.

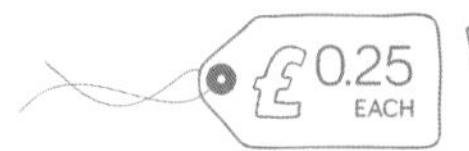

Coconut Cashew Cookies

125g softened **butter**

180g **soft brown sugar**

1 **egg**

140g **cashew nuts,** chopped

200g **GF self-raising flour**

1 teaspoon **xanthan gum**

50g **dessicated coconut**

1 teaspoon **vanilla extract**

2 tablespoons of **roasted chopped hazelnuts**

1. Preheat the oven to 180°C fan oven/200°C/gas 6. Line 2 baking trays.
2. Beat together the butter and sugar until light and creamy.
3. Add the egg and beat well.
4. Add the rest of the ingredients and gently mix together.
5. Turn the dough out onto a floured surface and divide into 16. Roll into balls, place on the baking sheet and press down until the cookie is approximately 1cm thick.
6. Sprinkle the hazelnuts over the cookies and press down lightly.
7. Bake in the oven for 12 minutes.

Like these cookies? Why not try some polenta cookies at noshbooks.com/polentacookies

White Chocolate and Raspberry Cookies

225g **butter**

225g **caster sugar**

170g **condensed milk**

350g **GF self-raising flour**

1 teaspoon **xanthan gum**

100g **white chocolate chips**

15g **freeze-dried raspberries**

NOTE: You can usually buy freeze-dried raspberries at Sainsburys and Waitrose.

1. Preheat the oven to 160°C fan oven/180°C/gas 5. Line 2 large baking trays.
2. Beat together the butter and sugar until light and fluffy.
3. Add the condensed milk and beat well.
4. Add the rest of the ingredients and mix in gently.
5. Wrap the dough in cling flim and leave in the fridge for 30 minutes.
6. Divide the dough into 24 pieces. Roll each into a ball, place on the baking sheet and squash down until each is approximately 1cm thick.
7. Bake in the oven for 18–20 minutes. The cookies should be lightly browned and chewy in the centres.

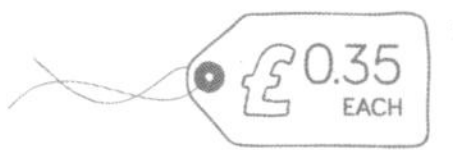

Almond and Ginger Cookies

4 **egg** whites

70g **crystallised ginger**, chopped (4 pieces)

400g **caster sugar**

200g **ground almonds**

200g **ground roasted hazelnuts**

2 teaspoons **lemon curd**

zest of 2 **lemons**

24 **whole almonds**

1. Preheat the oven to 160°C fan oven/180°C/gas 4. Prepare 2 lined baking trays.
2. Whisk the egg whites until they are stiff. Add the rest of the ingredients, apart from the whole almonds, and mix to a stiff paste.
3. Divide into 24 pieces and roll into balls. Place on the tray and squash down to about 1cm thick and place an almond on each cookie.
4. Bake in the oven for 16 minutes. Leave to cool on the tray. The cookies should be crisp on the outside and chewy on the inside.

Muesli Cookies

Dry ingredients

90g **GF oats**

150g **GF plain flour**

1 teaspoon **xanthan gum**

220g **caster sugar**

2 teaspoons **cinnamon**

35g **cranberries**

55g **chopped apricots**

70g **flaked almonds**

125g **butter**

2 tablespoons **golden syrup**

½ teaspoon **GF bicarbonate of soda**

1 tablespoon **warm water**

1. Preheat the oven to 150°C fan oven/170°C/gas 3. You will need 2 lined baking trays.
2. Put the dry ingredients in a large bowl and mix.
3. Gently melt the butter and syrup in a pan.
4. Mix together the bicarbonate of soda and warm water and add to the butter. The heat of the butter will cause the bicarbonate of soda to fizz a little.
5. Add to the dry ingredients and mix. The mixture will be quite stiff.
6. Take heaped dessertspoons of the mixture and squash to form balls. Place on the trays and squash down a little.
7. Bake in the oven for 20 minutes. Leave to cool on the trays.

Snickerdoodles

125g **butter**
100g **sugar**
1 **egg**
1 teaspoon **vanilla extract**
90g **ground almonds**
180g **GF self-raising flour**
1 teaspoon **xanthan gum**
1 teaspoon **GF baking powder**

2 tablespoons **sugar**
1 tablespoon **cinamon**

1. Preheat the oven to 160°C fan oven/180°C/gas 5. You will need 2 lined baking trays.
2. Beat the butter and sugar together until light and fluffy.
3. Add the egg and vanilla and beat well.
4. Add the almonds, flour, xanthan gum and baking powder and mix together.
5. Mix the sugar and cinnamon in a small bowl.
6. Take dessertspoons of the mixture, roll into balls and roll in the cinnamon mix. Place on the baking sheets.
7. Bake in the oven for 12 minutes.

Ginger Crunch Cookies

115g **butter**

90g/3 tablespoons **golden syrup**

350g **GF self-raising flour**

1 teaspoon **xanthan gum**

pinch **salt**

200g **soft brown sugar**

1 tablespoon **ground ginger**

1 teaspoon **bicarbonate of soda**

1 **egg**, beaten

4 pieces **stem ginger**, finely chopped

1. Preheat the oven to 160°C fan oven/180°C/gas 5. You will need a lined 20 x 30cm tray bake tin.
2. Melt the butter and syrup and leave to cool.
3. Put the flour, xanthan gum, salt, sugar, ginger and bicarbonate of soda in a large bowl and mix together.
4. Add the egg and the cooled butter mix to the dry ingredients and mix well.
5. Turn out onto a floured surface. Cut into 24 pieces and make each one into a ball. Place on lined baking trays. Press down with your fingers and then mark with a fork. Put some of the chopped stem ginger on the top of each cookie.
6. Bake in the oven for 14 minutes. The tops should be nicely browned.
7. Leave on the trays to cool and to set. The cookies should be crunchy.

TRAY BAKES

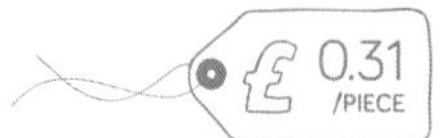

Millionaire's Shortbread

Shortbread

175g cold **butter**

80g **caster sugar**

250g **GF plain flour**

1 teaspoon **xanthan gum**

1 **egg**, beaten

1 tablespoon **water**

Centre

50g **butter**

90g **granulated sugar**

400g tin **condensed milk**

2 tablespoons **golden syrup**

Topping

200g **milk chocolate**

50g **white chocolate**

1. Preheat the oven to 180°C fan oven/200°C/gas 6. Grease and line a 20 x 30cm tray bake tin.

2. Put the butter, sugar, flour and xanthan gum in a food processor and whizz until you have something resembling breadcrumbs. Add the egg and water and pulse a few times until a soft dough is formed.

3. Remove from the food processor and press into the bottom of the tray. Bake in the oven for 25 minutes. Leave to completely cool.

4. Put the ingredients for the centre in a medium saucepan and gently bring to the boil, stirring frequently. Simmer gently for 5–8 minutes until the mixture turns golden brown. Take off the heat and leave to cool for 5 minutes. Pour over the shortbread and leave to set for 1 hour.

5. Melt the chocolate in a bowl over a pan of gently simmering water. Spread over the top of the caramel.

6. If you wish, you can melt some white chocolate and pipe in stripes across the melted milk chocolate. Take a skewer and pull across the stripes to make a feathered effect.

Cinnamon Apple Cake

150g softened **butter**, measure using packet

200g **sugar**

3 **eggs**

1 teaspoon **vanilla paste**

200g **GF self-raising flour**

1 teaspoon **xanthan gum**

1 teaspoon **GF baking powder**

2 tablespoons **cold water**

50g **ground almonds**

2 medium **cooking apples**, peeled and cut into thin wedges

2 tablespoons **granulated sugar**

1 teaspoon **ground cinnamon**

1. Preheat the oven to 180°C fan oven/200°C/gas 6. Grease and line a 20 x 30cm tray bake tin.
2. Beat together the butter and sugar until light and fluffy. Add the eggs, one at a time, beating in between each addition.
3. Add the vanilla paste, flour, xanthan gum, baking powder, water and ground almonds. Fold in gently.
4. Pour into the tray bake tin and spread out evenly. Press the apple wedges vertically into the cake. Mix together the sugar and cinnamon and sprinkle over the top.
5. Place in the oven for 30 minutes.
6. Leave to cool and cut into slices.

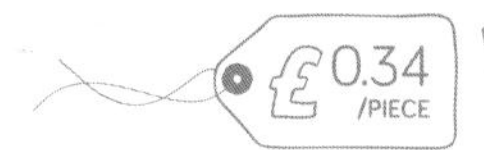

Granola Bars

These are great nutty bars and very moreish; a wonderful snack with a cup of tea.

- 50g **coconut chips**
- 50g **pinenuts**
- 25g **sesame seeds**
- 25g **sunflower seeds**
- 100g **roasted chopped hazelnuts**
- 40g **ground almonds**
- 100g **GF puffed rice**
- 100g **butter**
- 200g **dark brown sugar**
- 3 tablespoons **honey**

1. Preheat the oven to 160°C fan oven/180°C/gas 5. Grease and line a tray bake tin, approx 20 x 30cm.
2. Put the coconut chips, pinenuts, sesame seeds and sunflower seeds in a clean frying pan. Heat over a low heat and toast until everything begins to turn golden brown. Stir frequently. Tip into a large bowl.
3. Add the hazelnuts, almonds and puffed rice and mix well.
4. Put the butter, sugar and honey in a small saucepan and heat gently until the sugar is dissolved. Pour into the dry ingredients and mix well. Pour into the tray bake tin and flatten out evenly.
5. Bake in the oven for 30 minutes.
6. Leave to cool for at least 2 hours to allow the sugar to set. Cut into 24 pieces and store in a cake tin.

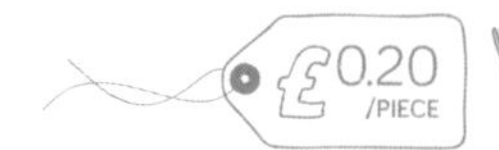

Macadamian Blondies

125g **butter**

200g **white chocolate**

280g **soft brown sugar**

150g **GF self-raising flour**

1 teaspoon **GF baking powder**

1 teaspoon **xanthan gum**

50g **dessicated coconut**

100g packet **macadamian nuts**, roughly chopped

3 **eggs**, beaten

1. Preheat the oven to 180°C fan oven/200°C/gas 6. Grease and line a 20 x 30cm baking tin.
2. Gently melt the butter and chocolate in a bowl over simmering water.
3. Put the dry ingredients in a large bowl. Add the eggs and mix well.
4. Add the melted butter and chocolate and mix well. Pour into the baking tin.
5. Place in the oven for 35 minutes, being careful not to overbake, as blondies, like brownies, should be a bit 'gooey' in the centre and crisp on the outside.
6. Leave to cool and cut into squares.

If you like blondies, you probably like brownies. Go to noshbooks.com/gfbrownies

Orange and Almond Slice

90g softened **butter**

110g **caster sugar**

1 **egg**

150g **GF self-raising flour**

1 teaspoon **xanthan gum**

300g **orange marmalade**

4 pieces **crystallised ginger**, chopped

1 **egg**, beaten

120g **flaked almonds**

60g **ground almonds**

icing sugar to dredge

1. Preheat the oven to 160°C fan oven/180°C/gas 5. Grease and line a 20 x 30cm tray bake tin.
2. Beat together the butter and sugar. Add the egg and beat well. Fold in the flour and xanthan gum.
3. Press evenly into the bottom of the tray bake tin.
4. Mix together the marmalade and ginger. Spread evenly over the dough.
5. Mix together the egg, ground almonds and flaked almonds. Spread evenly over the marmalade mix.
6. Bake in the oven for 40 minutes.
7. Allow to cool completely before cutting into slices and dredging with icing sugar.

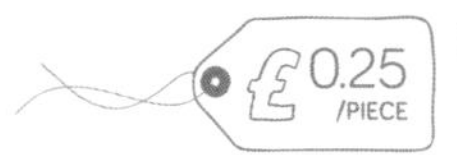

Coconut Cherry Slices

1 quantity of **chocolate pastry**, see page 11

350g **glacé cherries**, chopped
60g **icing sugar**
135g **dessicated coconut**
100g **melted butter**
125ml **condensed milk**

150g **dark chocolate**
25g **butter**

1. Preheat the oven to 180°C fan oven/200°C/gas 6. Grease and line a 20 x 30cm tray bake tin.
2. Make the pastry, see page 11.
3. Press into the base of the tin. Bake blind (see page 14) for 15 minutes. Take out the paper and baking beans and bake for a further 5 minutes. Leave to cool.
4. In a large bowl, mix together the cherries, icing sugar, and coconut. Add the melted butter and stir in the condensed milk. Spread over the cooled base and press down. Chill for 30 minutes.
5. Melt the chocolate and butter in a bowl over a pan of simmering water. Spread over the top of the coconut mix. Leave until it is almost set and then score the chocolate where you intend to cut, as this stops the chocolate cracking later.
6. When completely set, cut into squares.

Strawberry Shortbread

Shortbread

175g cold **butter**

80g **caster sugar**

250g **GF plain flour**

1 teaspoon **xanthan gum**

1 **egg**, beaten

1 tablespoon **water**

Topping

450g **mascarpone cheese**

100g **icing sugar**

juice of a **lemon**

300g **strawberries**, roughly chopped

50g **dark chocolate**

1. Preheat the oven to 180°C fan oven/200°C/gas 6. Grease and line a 20 x 30cm tray bake tin.

2. Put the butter, sugar, flour and xanthan gum in a food processor and whizz until you have something resembling breadcrumbs. Add the egg and water and pulse a few times until a soft dough is formed.

3. Remove from the food processor and press into the bottom of the tray. Bake in the oven for 25 minutes. Leave to cool completely.

4. Put the mascarpone, sugar and lemon in a large bowl and mix together until smooth. Add the strawberries and mix evenly. Spread over the cooled shortbread.

5. Melt the chocolate in a bowl over gently simmering water. Drizzle over the mascarpone mixture, see photo.

6. Leave in the fridge for at least 2 hours to set. Cut into squares.

Butterscotch Squares

You can eat these on their own as cakes, or dress them up with ice cream and some chopped nuts. Either way, they are yummy, the dark sugar giving a real butterscotch flavour. Quite different and very easy to make.

125g **butter**

250g **dark soft brown sugar**

2 **eggs**

150g **GF self-raising flour**

1 teaspoon **xanthan gum**

2 teaspoons **vanilla extract**

60g chopped **pecans**

1. Preheat the oven to 160°C fan oven/180°C/gas 4. Grease and line a tray bake tin, approx 20 x 30cm.
2. Melt the butter in a large saucepan, add the sugar and take off the heat. Allow to cool slightly.
3. Beat in the eggs.
4. Add the flour, xanthan gum, vanilla and pecans. Mix together gently.
5. Pour into the tin and bake in the oven for 30 minutes.
6. Cut into squares while still warm.
7. Serve with some ice cream and chopped nuts.

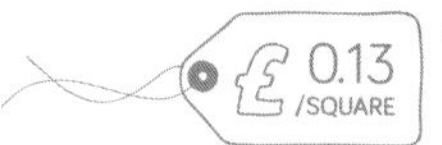

Banana Squares

125g softened **butter**, measure using packet

100g **caster sugar**

1 **egg**

4 tablespoons **golden syrup**

2 **ripe bananas**

180g **GF self-raising flour**

1 teaspoon **GF baking powder**

1 teaspoon **xanthan gum**

Topping

1 tablespoon **Demerara sugar**

2 tablespoons **roasted chopped hazelnuts**

1. Preheat the oven to 160°C fan oven/180°C/gas 5. Grease a 20 x 30cm tray bake tin.
2. Cream together the butter and sugar. Add the egg and beat well.
3. Add the syrup and beat well. Crush the bananas between your fingers and thumbs as you add to the mix. Beat well.
4. Add the flour, baking powder and xanthan gum and gently fold in.
5. Tip into the baking tray and spread out evenly. Mix together the sugar and nuts and sprinkle over the top. Bake in the oven for 25 minutes. The cake should spring back when gently pressed. Leave to cool before cutting into squares.

Crispy Rice Breakfast Bars

These will keep for up to a week in a tin and are good when you are on the run. Plus, they are pretty healthy.

397g tin **condensed milk**
150g **dried cranberries**
150g **raisins**
200g **GF oats**
50g **GF crispy rice**
50g **pumpkin seeds**

1. Preheat the oven to 150°C fan oven/170°C/gas 4. Grease and line a tray bake tin, approx 23 x 30cm.
2. Gently heat the condensed milk in a small pan.
3. Mix together the rest of the ingredients in a large bowl.
4. Pour in the warmed condensed milk. Mix together well. Transfer into the tray bake tin. Wet your hands with cold water and press down; this stops the mixture sticking to your fingers.
5. Bake in the oven for 30 minutes. Leave to cool completely before cutting into squares.

Turkish Delight Rocky Roads

Rocky Roads usually have Maltesers in them, but I have replaced them with Turkish Delight. Fry's claim that theirs are gluten-free, so watch out for it when you buy.

100g **butter**

225g **plain chocolate**

2 tablespoons **golden syrup**

2 tablespoons **caster sugar**

1 tablespoon **cocoa**

4 x 51g **bars Fry's Turkish Delight**, roughly chopped

100g **white chocolate chips**

100g **mini marshmallows**

225g **GF chocolate digestives**, roughly crushed

1. Line a 20 x 30cm tray bake tin.
2. Put the butter, chocolate, syrup and sugar in a small saucepan and gently heat until the butter and chocolate have melted. Leave to cool for 10 minutes or so.
3. Put the cocoa, Turkish Delight, chocolate chips, marshmallows and digestives in a large bowl and mix together. Add the contents of the saucepan and mix together until no dry bits remain.
4. Pour into the prepared tray bake tin and press down evenly.
5. Place in the fridge for at least an hour to set. Turn out onto a board and cut into 4cm squares.
6. Hide them in the fridge, so no one else knows where they are!

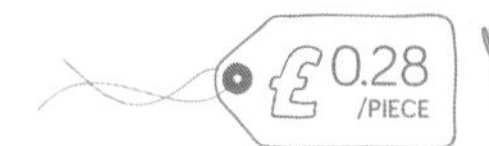

Golden Seed n' Nut Bars

150g **butter**, measure using packet

150g **caster sugar**

3 tablespoons **golden syrup**

80g **GF self-raising flour**

1 teaspoon **GF baking powder**

½ teaspoon **xanthan gum**

150g **dessicated coconut**

100g **pecans**, roughly chopped

60g **pumpkin seeds**

60g **sunflower seeds**

60g **pine nuts**

150g **raisins**

2 **eggs**

1. Preheat the oven to 160°C fan oven/180°C/gas 4. Grease and line a tray bake tin, approx 20 x 30cm.
2. Melt the butter, sugar and syrup gently in a pan. Leave to cool a little.
3. Mix together all the dry ingredients in a large bowl.
4. Add the eggs to the butter and sugar mix and beat well. Add to the dry ingredients and mix well.
5. Pour into the tray bake tin and smooth out.
6. Bake in the oven for 35 minutes. Leave to cool completely before cutting into squares.

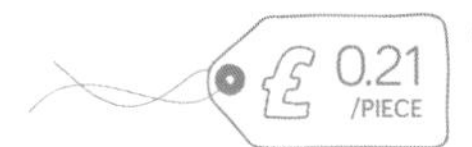

Chocolate Orange Tiffin

250g **GF chocolate digestive biscuits**

60g **dessicated coconut**

2 tablespoons **cocoa**

100g **ready-to-eat figs**

2 tablespoons **golden syrup**

125g **butter**

1 tablespoon **caster sugar**

grated rind of an **orange**

300g **milk chocolate**

1. Line a 20 x 30cm tray bake tin.
2. Put the biscuits in a poly bag and crush with a rolling pin. They don't need to be dust, you can leave some larger chunks in there. Place in a large bowl with the coconut, cocoa and figs and mix together.
3. Heat the syrup, butter and sugar in a small saucepan over a low heat. Once everything is melted, add the orange rind and mix.
4. Add to the large bowl and mix well. Pour into the tray bake tin and smooth out evenly. Press down to get everything together.
5. Put the chocolate in a bowl over a pan of simmering water and gently melt. Pour over the top of the biscuit mix and spread out evenly.
6. Place in the fridge for a couple of hours. Cut into squares and keep in the fridge until needed.

Honey Almond Slices

185g **butter**

125g **light brown sugar**

5 tablespoons **honey**

1 tablespoon **golden syrup**

200g **GF cornflakes**, lightly crushed

150g **ground almonds**

100g **toasted flaked almonds**

50g **GF plain flour**

1. Preheat the oven to 150°C fan oven/170°C/gas 4. Grease and line a 20 x 30cm tray bake tin.
2. Gently melt the butter, sugar, honey and syrup. Simmer gently for 2–3 minutes, or until the sugar dissolves.
3. In a large mixing bowl, mix together the crushed cornflakes, almonds, flaked almonds and flour. Pour in the butter, etc. and mix well.
4. Press into the tin and bake in the oven for 30 minutes.
5. Leave to completely cool before cutting into slices.

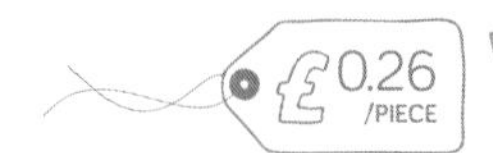

Figgy Flap Jacks

200g **butter**
175g **soft brown sugar**
150g **golden syrup**
350g **GF oats**
150g **figs**, chopped
100g **ready-to-eat apricots**, chopped

1. Preheat the oven to 170°C fan oven/190°C/gas 5. Line a 20 x 30cm tray bake cake tin.
2. Melt the butter in a large saucepan, along with the sugar and syrup.
3. Mix in the oats and fruits. Put the mixture in the tray bake tin and even out.
4. Bake in the oven for 35 minutes. The top should be nicely browned.

For a nutty shortbread recipe, head over to
noshbooks.com/nuttyshortbread

Chocolate Marble Cake

225g softened **butter**

225g **caster sugar**

4 **eggs**

100g **ground almonds**

175g **GF self-raising flour**

1 teaspoon **GF baking powder**

1 teaspoon **xanthan gum**

50g **white chocolate chips**

50g **dark chocolate chips**

2 tablespoons **milk**

1½ tablespoons **cocoa**

2½ tablespoons **water**

milk and white chocolate to drizzle over

1. Preheat the oven to 170°C fan oven/190°C/gas 5. Line a 20 x 30cm tray bake tin.
2. Beat the butter and sugar together until light and fluffy.
3. Add the eggs, one at a time, beating well between each addition.
4. Mix together the almonds, flour, baking powder, xanthan gum and chocolate chips. Add to the butter mix and fold in gently. Add the milk and gently mix.
5. Put half the mixture in blobs on the baking tray. Mix the cocoa and water together to a paste and add to the rest of the mixture. Mix until even. Add this mixture in blobs to the tray. Swirl around with a knife to randomly mix the plain and chocolate mixtures. Smooth over the surface.
6. Bake in the oven for 35 minutes. The cake should spring back lightly when gently pressed.
7. Once the cake is cooled, melt the chocolate in a bowl over simmering water. Drizzle the chocolate over. I put the melted chocolate in separate freezer bags and then snipped off one corner - makes a great icing bag.

Pineapple and Coconut Slices

130g **GF self-raising flour**

1 teaspoon **xanthan gum**

150g **soft brown sugar**

2 tablespoons **sunflower seeds**

2 tablespoons **sesame seeds**

70g chopped **macadamian nuts**

3 pieces **crystallised ginger**, chopped

50g **glacé cherries**, chopped

100g **dessicated coconut**

200g **tinned pineapple**, chopped and drained

150g **butter**, melted

2 **eggs**, beaten

Icing

200g **icing sugar**

50g softened **butter**

juice of a **lemon**

2 tablespoons **double cream**

40g **shredded coconut**

1. Preheat the oven to 160°C fan oven/180°C/gas 4. Grease and line a 20 x 30cm tray bake tin.
2. Put the flour, xanthan gum, sugar, sunflower seeds, sesame seeds, nuts, ginger, cherries and coconut in a large bowl. Stir together.
3. Add the pineapple, melted butter and beaten eggs and mix well.
4. Pour into the prepared baking tin and smooth out evenly.
5. Bake in the oven for 35 minutes. The top should be nicely browned and the cake bounce back a little when gently pressed.
6. Put the shredded coconut in a dry frying pan and gently toast until it begins to brown. Remove from the pan and chop a little.
7. To make the topping, beat together the icing, butter, lemon and cream until light and smooth. Spread over the cooled cake.
8. Sprinkle over the coconut topping. Cut the cake into approximately 24 pieces.

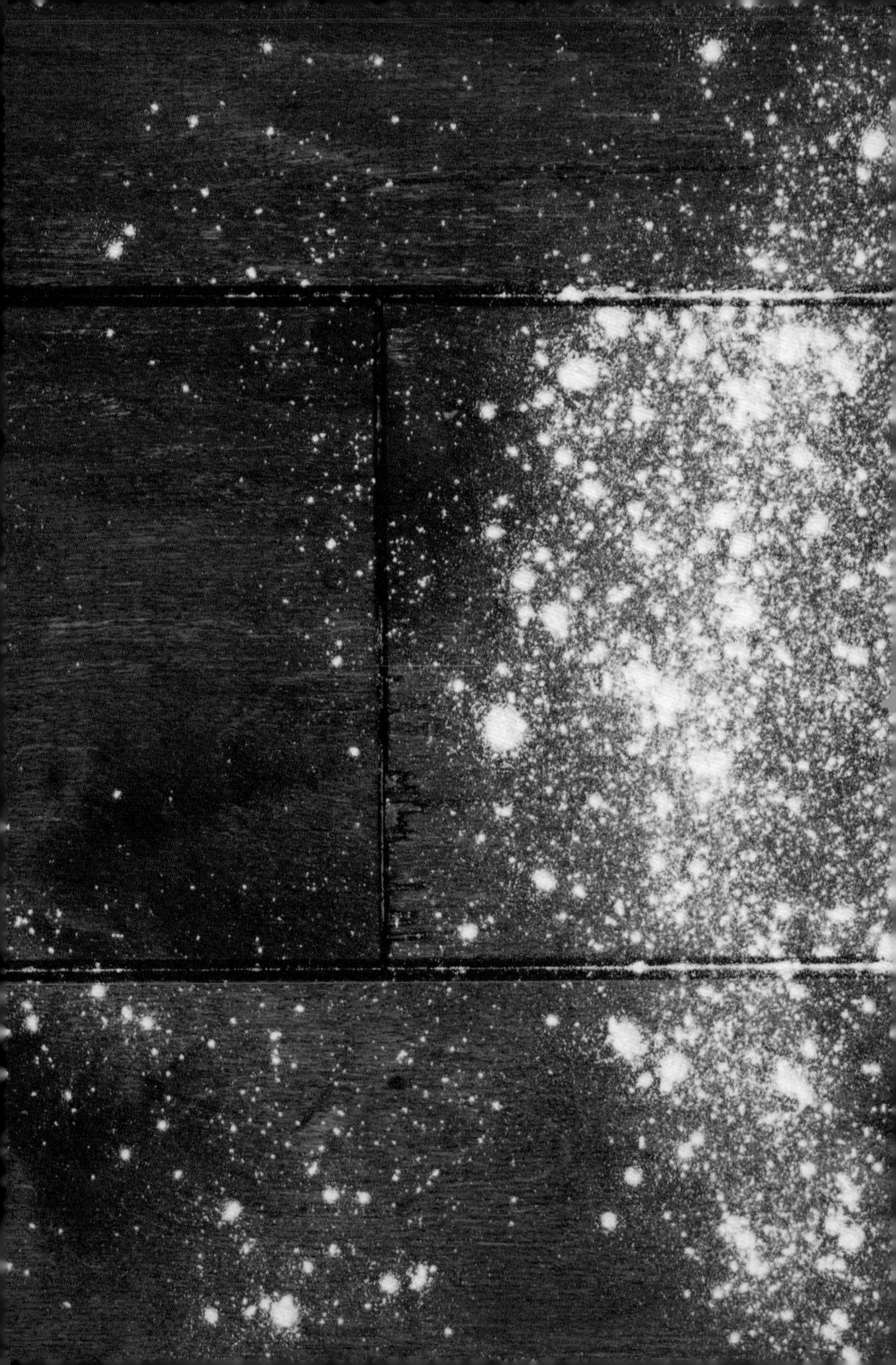

DESSERTS

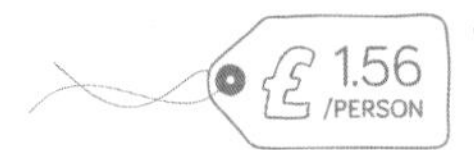

V

Mille-Feuille

1 quantity of **puff pastry**, see page 12

1 beaten **egg**

1 tablespoon **granulated sugar**

300ml **double cream**

150g **mascarpone**

2 teaspoons **vanilla paste**

raspberries

1. Make the pastry, see page 12.
2. Preheat the oven to 180°C fan oven/200°C/gas 6.
3. Roll out the pastry until it is 7mm thick. Cut into 8 equal rectangles and place on a lined baking sheet. Brush with beaten egg and sprinkle with granulated sugar. Place in the oven for 25 minutes. The tops should be nicely browned and the pastry risen.
4. Whip the cream until it is slightly thickened. Very gently fold in the mascarpone and the vanilla paste. Arrange on four of the pieces of pastry. Arrange the raspberries and top with the remaining sheets of pastry.

Berry and Apple Pie

Filling

2 medium **cooking apples**, peeled and cut into 2cm chunks

100ml **water**

100g **sugar**

450g pack of **frozen berries**

1 quantity of **almond shortcrust pastry**, see page 11

beaten **egg** to brush the pastry

1. To make the filling, place the apples in a large saucepan with the water and simmer until the apple begins to look a bit furry around the outsides. Take off the heat, add the sugar and the frozen fruit. Mix together and place in the pie dish.
2. Preheat the oven to 180°C fan oven/200°C/gas 6.
3. Make the pastry. Roll out on a sheet of floured cling film. Use the cling film to flip the pastry over the rolling pin and place over the pie dish. Trim and pinch the edges of the pie. Brush with the beaten egg.
4. Bake in the oven for 25 minutes.

Fancy another fruity dessert? Head over to noshbooks.com/pearcrumble

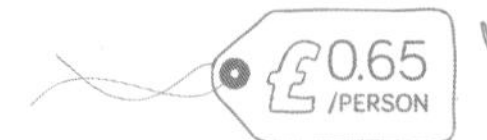

Apple Crumble

750g **Bramley apples**, peeled and cut into 2cm chunks

150ml **water**

90g **sugar**

2 **cloves**

Crumble topping

90g **ground almonds**

120g **coarse polenta**

120g **butter**

150g **soft brown sugar**

1. Preheat the oven to 160°C fan oven/180°C/gas 4.
2. Put the apples in a medium saucepan with approximately 150ml water. Simmer gently for 5 minutes. Add the sugar and the cloves and simmer for 2 minutes. Transfer into a medium-sized pie dish.
3. To make the crumble topping, put the ground almonds, polenta and butter in a food processor and whizz until you have something resembling breadcrumbs. Add the sugar and pulse a few times to mix.
4. Spread evenly over the apples.
5. Bake in the oven for 25–30 minutes. The top should be golden brown and crunchy.
6. Serve with fresh custard.

Treacle Tart

1 quantity of **basic shortcrust pastry**, see page 11

Filling

375g **golden syrup**

130g **GF breadcumbs**

60g **GF oats**

zest of a **lemon**

2 **eggs**, beaten

1. Preheat the oven to 180°C fan oven/200°C/gas 6.
2. Make the basic shortcrust pastry, see page 11.
3. Line a 20cm loose-bottomed flan tin. Bake blind for 15 minutes.
4. Meanwhile, mix together the filling ingredients.
5. Take the tart out of the oven and remove the paper and baking beans. Pour in the filling and spread out evenly. Bake in the oven for another 30 minutes.

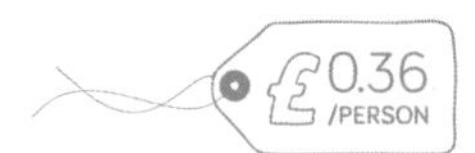

Pineapple Upside Down Pudding

butter to grease tin

272g **tin pineapple rings**

2 tablespoons **soft brown sugar**

150g **butter**

150g **caster sugar**

3 **eggs**

105g **GF self-raising flour**

1 teaspoon **GF baking powder**

1 teaspoon **xanthan gum**

60g **ground almonds**

1 tablespoon **cold water**

1. Preheat the oven to 180°C fan oven/200°C/gas 6. Grease a 20cm springform cake tin with plenty of butter. Sprinkle the bottom with the 2 tablespoons soft, brown sugar.
2. Arrange the pineapple rings on the bottom of the tin.
3. Beat together the butter and caster sugar until light and fluffy.
4. Add the eggs, one at a time, beating well between each addition.
5. Add the rest of the ingredients and gently mix together.
6. Put on top of the pineapple and smooth over evenly.
7. Bake in the oven for 30–35 minutes. The top should be lightly browned and the cake spring back when gently pressed.
8. Serve with custard.

Key Lime Pie

1 quantity of **sweet shortcrust pastry**, see page 11

4 **egg yolks**
zest of 4 **limes**
400g **condensed milk**
150ml **lime** juice

lime zest
crème fraîche

1. Preheat the oven to 180°C fan oven/200°C/gas 6. You will need either 6 individual flan dishes or a 20cm loose-bottomed flan tin.
2. Make the sweet pastry, see page 11.
3. Line the flan dishes. Bake blind for 15 minutes, remove the paper and beans and bake for a further 5 minutes.
4. Meanwhile, beat together the egg yolks and the lime zest. Add the condensed milk and beat well.
5. Add the lime juice and beat until the mixture thickens.
6. Take the pastry out of the oven and pour in the mixture.
7. Bake in the oven for 20 minutes for small pies and 25 minutes for larger ones.

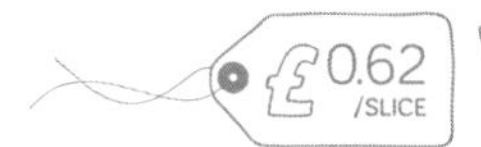

Baked Salted Caramel Cheesecake

1 quantity of **basic shortcrust pastry**, see page 11

Filling

400g **Philadelphia cream cheese**

400g **mascarpone cheese**

2 teaspoons **vanilla extract**

170g **caster sugar**

5 **eggs**

1 quantity of **salted caramel**, see page 16

1. Preheat the oven to 190°C fan oven/210°C/gas 7. Grease and line a 23cm springform tin.
2. Make the pastry. Roll half out to approximately 5mm thick and cut a circle slightly bigger than the base of the tin. Roll out the rest of the pastry to cover the sides of the tin. Allow it to come up over the top, this will stop the sides collapsing in.
3. Bake blind (see page 14) for 15 minutes.
4. Meanwhile, mix together the filling ingredients until smooth.
5. Take the pastry from the oven. Turn the oven down to 180°C fan oven/200°C/gas 6. Remove the greaseproof and baking beans and pour in the filling.
6. Bake in the oven for a further 45 minutes. Give the tin a little wobble; if it still appears runny, leave in the oven for a further 10 minutes, turning the oven down to 160°C fan oven/180°C/gas 5.
7. Once cooked, leave to cool. Trim off any excess pastry from the sides.
8. Make the caramel, see page 16.
9. Serve with caramel sauce or fruit.

Have you ever made an Austrian Curd Cheesecake? For the recipe go to noshbooks.com/curdcheesecake

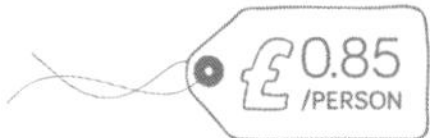

Caramel Pavlova

2 tablespoons **Demerara sugar**

4 **egg whites**

225g **caster sugar**

200g **milk chocolate**

300ml **double cream**

300g **raspberries**

Caramel Sauce

100g **butter**

4 tablespoons **soft brown sugar**

75ml **cream**

1. Preheat the oven to 150°C fan oven/170°C/gas 4. Line a large baking sheet.
2. Spread the 2 tablespoons of Demerara sugar on a non-stick sheet and place under the grill. Watch carefully until the sugar caramelises. Leave to cool and then crush the sugar with a spoon, leaving some larger 'crumbs'.
3. Whisk the egg whites in a clean bowl. Once they are quite stiff, gradually add the caster sugar and beat until the mixture is stiff and the sugar is dissolved. Rub between your fingers and thumb to check. Stir in the caramelised sugar.
4. Spread on the baking tray and form into a circle.
5. Place in the oven for 1 hour. Switch off the oven and leave the meringue in for a further 15 minutes. Take out of the oven and leave to cool.
6. Make the caramel sauce by putting the ingredients in a small pan and gently bringing to the boil. Simmer for 3 minutes and then leave to cool.
7. Melt the chocolate in a pan over simmering water. Drizzle over the meringue, see photo.
8. Whip the 300ml cream and spread over the centre of the pavlova. Add the raspberries and drizzle over the cooled caramel.

If you like this Pavlova, why not try this almond and pear Pavlova at noshbooks.com/pearpavlova

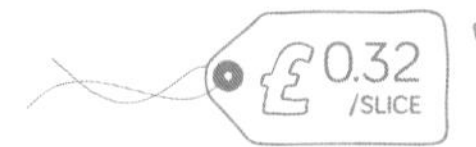

Hazelnut Chocolate Torte

200g **dark chocolate**
175g **butter**
175g **caster sugar**
5 **eggs**
1 tablespoon **cocoa**
100g **ground roasted hazelnuts**

1. Preheat the oven to 160°C fan oven/180°C/gas 5. Grease and line a 23cm round cake tin.
2. Melt the chocolate in a bowl over a pan of simmering water. Leave to cool slightly.
3. Beat the butter and sugar until light and fluffy. Separate the eggs. Add the egg yolks, one at a time, beating in between each addition. Stir in the chocolate, cocoa and the hazelnuts.
4. Beat the egg whites in a separate bowl until they are stiff. Add half to the chocolate mixture and carefully fold in; this loosens the mixture a little. Add the other half and carefully fold in. Pour into the cake tin and gently spread out.
5. Bake in the oven for 55 minutes. The cake should spring back slightly when pressed. Take out of the oven and leave in the tin to cool.
6. Serve with a little cream.

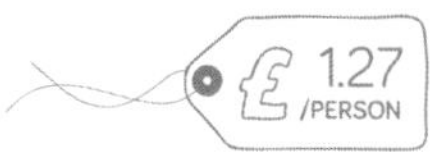

Mint Chocolate Mousse with Strawberries and Cream

This is quite rich, so, if you are making it as part of a 3 course meal, it will easily stretch to 8 people.

Mousse

200g **Green and Blacks minted chocolate**

3 **egg** whites

300ml **double cream**

200g **fresh strawberries**

300ml **double cream**

1. Melt the chocolate in a bowl over a pan of gently simmering water. Leave to cool slightly.
2. Whisk the egg whites until light and fluffy.
3. In a separate bowl, beat the cream until it is thickened.
4. Gently fold the chocolate into the cream and then gently fold in the egg whites. Once thoroughly mixed, spoon into 6 individual bowls.
5. Leave in the fridge for 1 hour to set.
6. Beat the other 300ml of cream until thick. Place a blob on top of each dish. Cut the strawberries into smaller pieces and place on top.

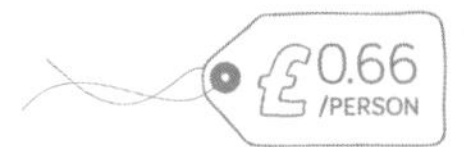

Raspberry Roulade

This is best eaten the day it is made, as the moisture from the cream and raspberries will make the roulade a bit soggy. However, it is still delicious even when soggy.

4 **egg whites**

225g **caster sugar**

1 teaspoon **almond essence**

60g **ground almonds**

300g **fresh raspberries**

300ml **double cream**

1. Preheat the oven to 150°C fan oven/170°C/gas 4. Grease and line a Swiss roll tin, approx 30 x 40cm.
2. Put the egg whites in a clean bowl and whisk until they are really stiff. Continue to whisk while gradually adding the sugar and whisk until smooth and glossy.
3. Add the almond essence and the almonds and gently stir in. Pour onto the Swiss roll tin and gently even out.
4. Place in the oven for 30 minutes.
5. Take out of the oven and cover with a clean piece of greaseproof paper and then cover with a lightly damp tea towel. Leave to cool completely.
6. Put the damp tea towel on a work surface and on top place a clean sheet of greaseproof paper and sprinkle with icing sugar. Turn the roulade out onto the paper. Gently peel off the greaseproof it has been cooked in.
7. Beat the cream until it is stiff, but be careful not to overbeat. Spread over the roulade and sprinkle over the raspberries.
8. Using the tea towel and the greaseproof to grip, gently roll up the roulade as tight as possible. It may crack a little on the surface but that does not matter. Dredge over some icing sugar and serve.

We have got a simply splendid roulade recipe for you to try at noshbooks.com/roulade

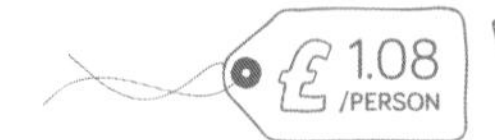

Chocolate Cherry Sundaes

2 **eggs**
60g **caster sugar**
35g **GF plain flour**
35g **ground almonds**
2 tablespoons **cocoa**

4 tablespoons **white rum**

Cheats Custard

150ml **milk**
300ml **double cream**
3 **egg** yolks
2 tablespoons **sugar**
1 teaspoon **vanilla bean paste**
2 tablespoons **cornflour**

packet good quality **cherry pie filling**
300ml **double cream**
1 **flake bar**

1 Preheat the oven to 200°C fan oven/220°C/gas 7. Grease and line a Swiss roll tin, approx 23 x 30cm.

2 Put the eggs and sugar in a bowl and whisk until pale and thick. Gently fold in the flour, almonds and cocoa. Pour into the lined tin and spread out evenly.

3 Bake in the oven for 10–12 minutes. The cake should spring back a little when gently pressed. Leave to cool, remove from the tin and remove the greaseproof paper.

4 Break up the cake and place on a plate. Drizzle over the rum.

5 To make the custard, bring the milk and cream to the boil. Mix together the egg yolks, sugar, vanilla paste and cornflour in a bowl. Pour over the heated milk and quickly stir. The custard should thicken. If it doesn't, put it back into the pan and heat very gently until it thickens, taking care not to heat it too quickly as it will curdle. Cool a little.

6 Beat the cream.

7 Layer the cake, cherries, custard and cream in the sundae dishes. Top with some cream and sprinkle over the crumbled flake.

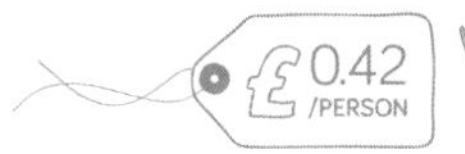

Banoffee Pie

½ quantity of **sweet pastry**, see page 11

3 **bananas**, sliced

Toffee Filling

50g **butter**

90g **soft brown sugar**

400g **tin Carnation milk**

2 tablespoons **golden syrup**

300ml **double cream**

dark chocolate, cold from the fridge

1. Preheat the oven to 200°C fan oven/220°C/gas 7. You will need a 20cm loose-bottomed flan ring.
2. Roll the pastry out and line the flan ring, placing it on a baking tray. Bake blind for 20 minutes. Remove the baking beans. Turn the oven down to 180°C fan oven/200°C/gas 6 and bake for a further 5 minutes.
3. Let the pastry cool a little and then fill with the sliced bananas.
4. Put the ingredients for the toffee filling in a small saucepan and gently bring to the boil. Turn down to simmer for about 5 minutes until the mixture changes colour to a more golden brown. Pour over the bananas and leave to cool.
5. Whip the cream and spread over the top.
6. Using a bar of dark chocolate, take a sharp knife and scrape across the back to make some shavings. Sprinkle over the top.

Lemon Meringue Pie

1 quantity of **basic shortcrust pastry**, see page 11

125ml **lemon juice**

juice of an **orange**

2 tablespoons **cornflour**

100g **caster sugar**

zest of 2 **lemons**

85g **butter**

3 **egg yolks** + 1 **egg**

Meringue

3 **egg whites**

150g **caster sugar**

1. Preheat the oven to 200°C fan oven/220°C/gas 7. You will need a 20cm flan ring.
2. Roll out the pastry and line the flan ring. Trim the edges. Bake blind for 20 minutes. Remove the baking beans and bake for a further 5 minutes.
3. Meanwhile, make the filling. Mix the lemon and orange juice together and add water to make 200ml liquid. Add to the cornflour, sugar, lemon rind and butter and place in a small pan. Heat gently until the mixture thickens.
4. Take off the heat. Beat together the egg yolks and the egg and add to the pan. Beat well and heat gently until it thickens. Do not bring to the boil.
5. Pour into the baked pastry case.
6. Whisk the egg whites until they are stiff. Gradually add the sugar, whisking all the time, and whisk until the meringue is stiff and shiny. Gently place on top of the lemon mixture.
7. Turn the oven down to 160°C fan oven/180°C/gas 5. Put the pie in the oven for 25 minutes. The meringue should be very lightly browned.
8. Leave to cool before cutting.

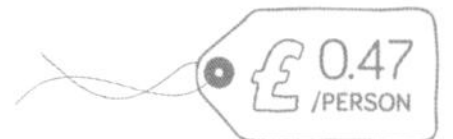

Melting Pots

200g **dark chocolate**

125g **butter**

150g mug **soft brown sugar**

4 **eggs**

1 teaspoon **vanilla extract**

90g **GF self-raising** flour

1/2 teaspoon **xanthan gum**

1/2 teaspoon **GF baking powder**

1. Preheat the oven to 180°C fan oven/200°C/gas 6. Grease 6 ramekin dishes with butter.
2. Melt the chocolate in a bowl over a pan of simmering water. Leave to cool slightly.
3. Beat together the butter and sugar until light and fluffy.
4. Add the eggs, one at a time, beating well between each addition.
5. Add the chocolate and vanilla and stir in.
6. Fold in the flour, xanthan gum and baking powder.
7. Divide between the ramekin dishes; they should not be more than 2/3rds full. Bake in the oven for 20 minutes. Serve whilst still hot. Ice cream works really well with the hot, soft, gooey centres.

French Apple Tart

1 quantity of **sweet pastry**, see page 11

2 **cooking apples**

2 tablespoons **caster sugar**

4 **Granny Smith apples**

Glaze

4 tablespoons **apricot jam**

1 tablespoon **water**

1. Preheat the oven to 180°C fan oven/200°C/gas 6.
2. Make the pastry and turn out onto a sheet of floured cling film. Roll until the pastry is approximately 5mm thick. Use the cling film to help the pastry over the rolling pin and transfer into a 20cm loose-bottomed flan tin.
3. Bake blind for 15 minutes, see page 14.
4. Meanwhile, peel and chop the cooking apples and place in a pan with ½ mug water. Simmer gently until the apples fall apart. Add the caster sugar and press through a sieve. Peel and slice the Granny Smiths, keeping them covered until needed.
5. Take the tart out of the oven. Remove the paper and baking beans. Pour the apple purée into the bottom. Arrange the sliced apple, see photo.
6. Return to the oven for 25 minutes.
7. Heat the apricot jam and the water in a small pan and mix until really smooth.
8. Take the tart out of the oven and spread the glaze over. Put back in the oven for 10 minutes. Leave to cool before slicing.

Fancy another tart? Then head over to noshbooks.com/peartart

Mississippi Mud Pie

1 quantity of **sweet pastry**, see page 11

Filling

30g **golden syrup**

50g **butter**

150g **dark chocolate**

6 **eggs**

300g **soft brown sugar**

1 teaspoon **vanilla extract**

300ml **double cream**

1. Preheat the oven to 200°C fan oven/220°C/gas 7. You will need 23cm flan dish or ring.
2. Make the pastry. Line the flan dish/ring. Bake blind for 15 minutes. Take the baking beans out and bake for a further 5 minutes.
3. Meanwhile, make the filling. Gently melt together the syrup, butter and chocolate. Leave to cool slightly.
4. In a large bowl, whisk together the eggs and sugar and add the vanilla.
5. Pour the chocolate into the egg mixture and whisk.
6. Turn the oven down to 150°C fan oven/170°C/gas 3.
7. Pour the chocolate mix into the flan dish and bake in the oven for 45 minutes. The pie will still wobble a little.
8. Once the pie is completely cooled, whip the cream and decorate the top. Add some grated chocolate if you wish.

sherry or brandy
gentle heat,
e sugar and
Stir con-
until

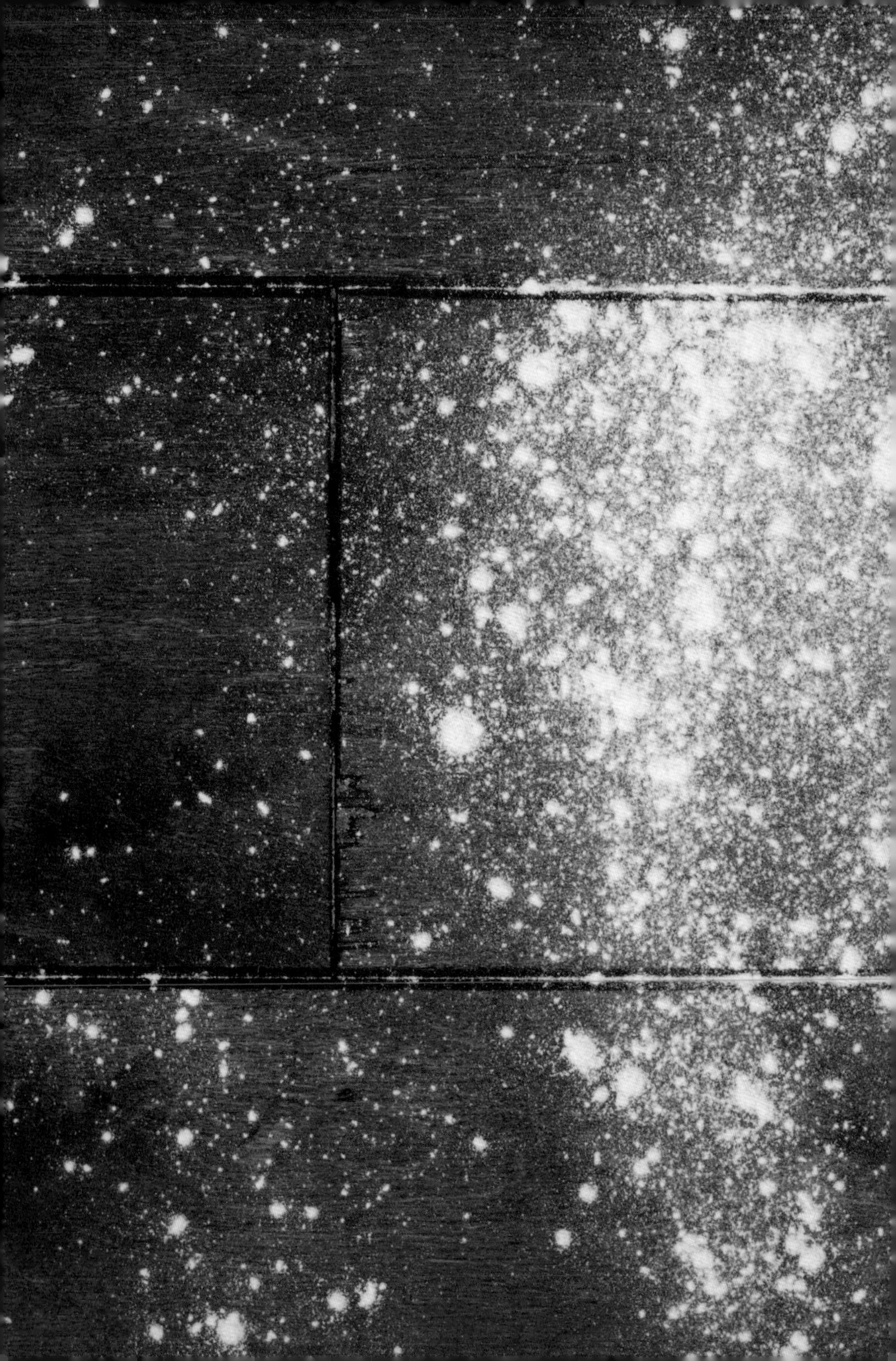

SAVOURY BAKES

Salmon Koulibiac

You do not need to make the fish decoration, but it can be fun. Just make sure it is not too thick.

1 quantity of **chickpea pastry**, see page 11

Filling

½ mug **wild rice**, cooked

2 tablespoons **oil**

3 **salmon steaks**

1 **onion**, chopped

4 **mushrooms**, chopped

2 tablespoons freshly chopped **parsley**

2 **eggs**, beaten

egg, beaten to brush

salad to serve

1. Preheat the oven to 180°C fan oven/200°C/gas 6.
2. Cook the wild rice in 2 mugs of boiling water for about 25 minutes.
3. Heat the oil in a large frying pan. Cook the salmon for 2–3 minutes each side until it is just cooked. Place in a large bowl and flake. Add to the cooked rice. Season well with salt and pepper.
4. Fry the onions and mushrooms until they are lightly browned. Add to the salmon, along with the parsley and the 2 eggs. Leave to cool while you make the pastry.
5. Make the pastry, see page 11.
6. Roll out the pastry into an oblong 5mm thick. Place the filling on one side of the oblong. Wet the edges of the pastry. Use the cling flim to help to fold the other half of the pastry over. Trim, being careful not to cut through the cling flim, and pinch the edges together.
7. Use the cling film again to transfer the pie to a large baking tray. Brush with the beaten egg.
8. Bake in the oven for 35 minutes.
9. Serve with salad.

For another pie recipe, head over to notebooks.com/lambpie

Tuna Empanadas

5 medium **potatoes**
2 tablespoons **paprika**
2 tablespoons **olive oil**

Filling

1 tablespoon **oil**
½ **onion**, chopped
2 **tomatoes**, chopped
2 tablespoons **sundried tomato purée**
1 **roasted red pepper**, chopped
2 tablespoons freshly chopped **parsley**
175g **tuna**, drained

1 quantity of **basic shortcrust pastry**, see page 11

egg to brush

salad and **dressing,** see page 188

1. Preheat the oven to 180°C fan oven/200°C/gas 6.
2. Cut the potatoes into fat chips. Put on a large baking tray and sprinkle with the paprika, oil and salt and pepper. Mix everything together and spread out the chips. Place in the oven for 35–40 minutes.
3. To make the filling, heat the oil in a large frying pan and add the onion. Fry until it begins to brown. Add the tomatoes and the tomato purée and fry until the tomatoes begin to soften. Add the rest of the filling ingredients and mix together. Take off the heat and season well with salt and pepper. Leave to cool a little.
4. Make the pastry, see page 11. Put some cling film on the surface and lightly dust with flour. Roll out the pastry until it is about 5mm thick. Cut out 8 x 10cm rounds.
5. Place 4 of the rounds on a lined baking tray. Divide the filling between them. Wet the edges with a little water to help the two layers stick together. Place the other rounds on top and pinch together. Brush with the beaten egg.
6. Bake in the oven for 25 minutes.
7. Serve with the chips and salad.

Stilton and Caramelised Onion Pie

1 quantity of **puff pastry**, see page 12

50g **butter**

1 tablespoon **olive oil**

2 **onions**, sliced

1kg **new potatoes**, sliced

150g **Stilton cheese**, grated

100g **Gruyère cheese**, grated

1 tablespoon freshly chopped **parsley**

1 tablespoon freshly chopped **basil**

½ teaspoon grated **nutmeg**

250ml **double cream**

beaten egg to brush the pastry

1 Preheat the oven to 200°C fan oven/220°C/gas 7.

2 Make the pastry, see page 12. Leave covered in the fridge.

3 Heat the butter and oil in a large frying pan. Fry the onions on a medium heat until they are browned and caramelised. This may take as long as 10 minutes.

4 Put the potatoes in boiling water and simmer gently for 10 minutes. Drain and put in a pie dish.

5 Mix in the onions, cheeses, herbs and nutmeg and season well. Arrange over the potatoes.

6 Pour the cream over the dish.

7 Roll out the pastry and put over the pie. Brush with the beaten egg. Bake in the oven for 20–25 minutes. The crust should be crisp and lightly browned.

Chicken and Mushroom Pie with Thyme and Lemon Pastry

4 medium-sized **potatoes**, cut into 3cm chunks

2 tablespoons **olive oil**

1 quantity of **basic shortcrust pastry** (p9)

zest of a **lemon**

1 tablespoon freshly chopped **thyme**

1 tablespoon **oil**

3 **chicken breasts**, cut into bite-sized pieces

2 tablespoons **GF plain flour**

300ml **water** + GF **chicken stock pot**

1 bunch **spring onions**

250g **mushrooms**, sliced

beaten **egg** to glaze

200g **grean beans**

1. Preheat the oven to 180°C fan oven/200°C/gas 6. You will need a lined 20 x 30cm tray bake tin.
2. Put the potatoes on a roasting tray, drizzle over the oil, season with salt and pepper and mix together. Put in the oven.
3. To make the pastry, see page 11. Add the lemon zest and thyme to the dry ingredients of the pastry before mixing.
4. Heat the 1 tablespoon oil in a large frying pan or wok. Add the chicken and fry until it begins to brown. Add the flour and mix well. Add the water and stock pot and bring to the boil. The sauce should thicken.
5. Add the spring onions and mushrooms. Bring back to the boil. Transfer the chicken mix into a pie dish.
6. Roll out the pastry. Brush the edges of the dish with water (helps the pastry to stick), put the pastry over and cut to size. Pinch the edges and brush the top with some beaten egg.
7. Bake in the oven for 30 minutes.
8. Meanwhile, put the beans on to cook. Drain and return to the pan until needed.

 Fancy another pie recipe? Head over to noshbooks.com/ardennespie

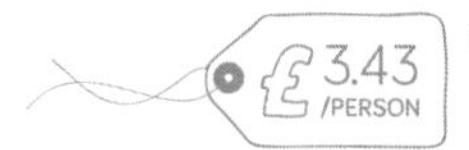

Beef and Red Wine Pie

2 tablespoons **oil**

2 **onions**, sliced

200g **pancetta lardons**

800g **beef stewing steak**

3 tablespoons **GF plain flour**

150ml **red wine**

600ml **water**

2 **beef stock cubes** + 1 teaspoon **dried thyme**

3 **bay leaves**

2 **carrots**, sliced

250g **chestnut mushrooms**, sliced

1 quantity **basic shortcrust pastry**, see page 11

1 **egg**, beaten, to brush the pastry

1 **head of broccoli**

6 medium **potatoes,** peeled and cut into 3cm chunks

1 Preheat the oven to 180°C fan oven/200°C/gas 6.

2 Heat the oil in a large 'hob to oven' casserole dish. Add the onions and fry until they begin to soften. Add the pancetta lardons and fry until they begin to brown. Add the beef and fry until the outsides are no longer pink.

3 Add the flour and mix well. Add the wine, water and stock. Bring to the boil and the sauce should thicken. Add the herbs, carrots and mushrooms and season well with salt and pepper.

4 Put the lid on and place in the oven for 1½ hours. Once cooked, pour into a casserole dish.

5 To make the pastry, see page 11.

6 Roll out on a piece of floured cling film until it is the size to cover your casserole dish. Wet the edges of the dish with water. Transfer the pastry over the top. Trim the edges and crimp them. Brush the pastry with beaten egg and place in the oven for 45 minutes. The top should be nicely browned and the pastry crisp.

7 Meanwhile, put the potatoes into a pan of boiling water along with the broccoli stems, simmer for 5 minutes and then add the rest of the broccoli for a further 5 minutes. Drain and mash.

Beef and Onion Pie with Cheese Pastry

Filling

1 tablespoon **olive oil**

2 **red onions**, sliced

500g **minced beef**

1 tablespoon **GF plain flour**

4 sprigs **thyme**

1 teaspoon **dry mustard**

2 tablespoons **balsamic vinegar**

2 tablespoons **tomato purée**

1 mug **water**

1 quantity of **cheese pastry**, see page 11

1. Preheat the oven to 180°C fan oven/200°C/gas 6.
2. Heat the oil in a large frying pan or wok. Add the onions and fry until they begin to soften. Add the meat and fry until no longer pink.
3. Add the flour and mix well. Add the rest of the filling ingredients and season well with salt and pepper. Leave to simmer while you make the pastry, then put in the pie dish.
4. Make the pastry. Put a piece of cling film on the work surface and dust with flour. Squash the pastry into a ball and roll until it is about 5mm thick. Use the cling film to help lift the pastry over the rolling pin. Wet the edges of the pie dish and place the pastry over. Cut to size, crimp the edges and pierce a hole in the centre to let the steam out.
5. Brush with the beaten egg.
6. Place in the oven for 30 minutes. The pastry should be nicely browned.
7. Serve with greens and mini roasts.

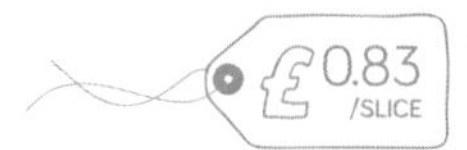

Smoked Mackerel Tart with Apple Salad

1 quantity of **basic shortcrust pastry**, see page 11

Tart Ingredients

25g **butter**, measure using packet

1 tablespoon **olive oil**

2 **red onions**, sliced

200g **smoked mackerel**

4 **eggs**

300ml **crème fraîche**

2 tablespoons freshly chopped **parsley**

2 teaspoons **wholegrain mustard**

Salad

2 **little gem lettuces**, finely sliced

1 **green apple**, cored and cut into thin sticks

3 **spring onions**, sliced lengthways

salt and **pepper**

juice of ½ **lemon**

2 tablespoons **olive oil**

1. Preheat the oven to 180°C fan oven/200°C/gas 6.
2. Make the pastry, see page 11. Roll out on some floured cling film. Use the cling film to tip the pastry over the rolling pin and place in a flan dish. Press into the dish and trim off the edges. Leave in the fridge until you are ready to use.
3. Heat the butter and oil in a large frying pan and fry the onions until they are caramelised; this may take as long as 10 minutes. Keep stirring the onions to ensure they don't burn. Season well with salt and pepper.
4. Peel the skin off the mackerel and flake the fish. Mix with the onions and arrange in the flan dish.
5. Beat the eggs in a large jug and season with salt and pepper. Add the crème fraîche, parsley and mustard and mix well.
6. Put the flan dish on a baking tray. Slowly pour over the egg mixture, allowing the air bubbles to surface. Place in the oven for 35 minutes. Turn the oven down to 160°C fan oven/180°C/gas 5 and cook for a further 10 minutes.
7. Mix together the salad ingredients and serve with the tart.

sugar
yolks and
essence to flavour.
for about ½ hour
brown
on the

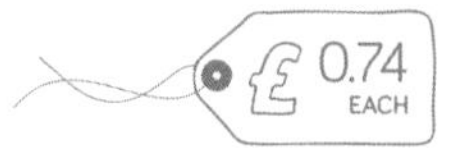

Mini Chorizo Quiches

1 quantity of **basic shortcrust pastry,** see page 11

1 tablespoon **olive oil**

1 **onion**, chopped

150g **diced chorizo**

100g **spinach**, chopped

4 **eggs**, beaten

200ml **crème fraîche**

100ml **double cream**

50g grated **Cheddar cheese**

50g **pine nuts**

1. Preheat the oven to 180°C fan oven/200°C/gas 6. You will need 6 mini flan tins or 1 x 20cm flan dish.
2. Roll out the pastry and line the flan tins. Bake blind for 10 minutes (see page 14). Remove the baking beans and bake for a further 5 minutes.
3. Meanwhile, heat the oil in a large frying pan and fry the onions and chorizo until they begin to brown.
4. Take the pan off the heat and add the spinach.
5. Mix the eggs, crème fraîche and cream together in a bowl.
6. Take the pastry cases out of the oven. Divide the chorizo mix between them and spread it out. Carefully pour the egg mix in until the cases are full.
7. Sprinkle over the cheese and then the pine nuts.
8. Bake in the oven for 25 minutes. If you are just using one large flan dish, you will need to cook for 5–10 minutes longer.

Cheese Scones

If you don't eat these straight away, whilst they are still warm, pop them in the microwave for a few seconds to bring them back to their best.

140g **butter**, measure using packet

400g **GF self-raising flour**

1 teaspoon **xanthan gum**

1 teaspoon **GF baking powder**

½ teaspoon **paprika**

1 teaspoon finely chopped **rosemary**

80g grated **Gruyère cheese**

1 beaten **egg** + **milk** to make up to 260ml

beaten **egg** to brush

1. Preheat the oven to 180°C fan oven/200°C/gas 6. Grease a baking tray.
2. Put the butter, flour, xanthan gum, baking powder, paprika and rosemary in a food processor. Blitz until you have something resembling breadcrumbs.
3. Add the cheese and pulse a couple of times.
4. Add the egg and milk and pulse a few times until a dough is formed.
5. Turn out onto a floured surface and squash into a ball. Press down until the dough is approximately 5cm thick. Cut out rounds. Place on the baking sheet and brush the tops with the other beaten egg.
6. Bake in the oven for 15 minutes.

Ron's Yorkshire Puddings

We have called these Ron's Yorkshire Puddings as he is the self-appointed Yorkshire pudding expert in our family, despite the fact that he is a Geordie and I am actually from Yorkshire!

190g **GF white bread flour**

1 teaspoon **GF bicarbonate of soda**

5 **eggs**

5 tablespoons **milk**

225ml cold **water**

½ teaspoon **salt**

white Flora/Trex

1. Preheat the oven to 220°C fan oven/ 240°C/gas 9, or as high as your oven will go!
2. Place blobs/1 teaspoon of white Flora in the bottoms of a deep, 12 hole, muffin tray. Place in the oven.
3. Mix the pudding ingredients in a food processor, or whisk with a hand-held whisk. Don't overbeat, but mix until smooth. Add enough water to make the mixture the consistency of single cream.
4. Once the fat in the oven is smoking, take the tin out of the oven and quickly add the pudding mix. The fat should sizzle as the mixture goes in.
5. Place in the oven for 15 minutes, or until very browned.

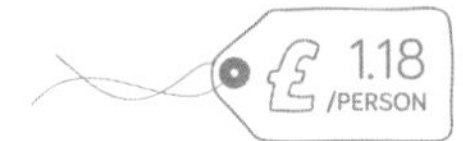

Corn Tortillas

Tortillas

200g **GF white bread flour**

180g **fine polenta**

2 teaspoons **xanthan gum**

1 teaspoon **GF baking powder**

2 teaspoons **soft brown sugar**

1 teaspoon **salt**

300ml **cold water**

oil to fry

Filling

Little Gem lettuce

8 slices **pastrami**

2 sliced **tomatoes**

1 sliced **avocado**

Dressing

4 tablespoons **GF mayo**

4 **sundried tomatoes**, chopped

salt and **pepper**

1. Put the dry ingredients for the tortillas in a food processor. Pulse a couple of times to mix. Add the water and pulse a few times more until a soft dough is formed.
2. Turn onto a floured surface. Divide the dough into 8 pieces. Roll each one out as thinly as possible. It can help either to roll the dough on floured cling film in order to help move the tortilla once rolled, or use a 'cake mover'.
3. Heat a little oil in a medium frying pan and gently fry each tortilla on both sides until lightly browned and cooked through.
4. Mix together the dressing ingredients and fill the tortillas. Roll up ready to eat.

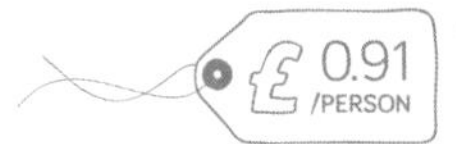

Thin Crust Pizza

Base

1 tablespoon **honey**

150ml **warm water**

1½ teaspoons **dried yeast**

200g **GF bread flour**

1 teaspoon **GF baking powder**

1 teaspoon **xanthan gum**

½ teaspoon **salt**

1 **egg**

2 tablespoons **olive oil**

½ teaspoon **cider vinegar**

3 tomatoes, **chopped**

2 tablespoons **sundried tomato purée**

1 tablespoon freshly chopped **basil**

125g **mozzarella cheese**, sliced

salami

or whatever toppings you like

1. Mix together the honey and warm water and then sprinkle over the yeast. Mix together and leave in a warm place for about 7 minutes, or until it bubbles up a little.
2. Mix the flour, baking powder, xanthan gum and salt together in a large bowl.
3. Beat the egg, olive oil and cider vinegar together.
4. Once the yeast has begun to bubble, place in the flour, along with the egg mix and mix together until smooth. The dough will be quite soft.
5. Grease a large baking tray. With floured hands, form the dough into a ball and place on the baking tray. Roll out the dough with a floured rolling pin, until it is round and approximately 5mm thick. Place in a warm place for 45 minutes to prove.
6. Meanwhile, prepare the pizza topping. Fry the tomatoes until they begin to soften. Add the tomato purée and the chopped basil. Set to one side until needed.
7. Preheat the oven to 200°C fan oven/220°C/gas 7.
8. After the proving time, put the pizza base in the oven for 7 minutes.
9. Spread the tomato mixture over the base and arrange the toppings.
10. Bake in the oven for a further 10 minutes.

Smoked Paprika Tortilla Chips

280g **GF plain flour**
1 teaspoon **salt**
135g **fine polenta**
1 teaspoon **GF baking powder**
1 teaspoon **xanthan gum**
500ml **vegetable oil**
250ml **warm water**

2 teaspoons **smoked paprika** (optional)

vegetable oil to fry

1. Put the ingredients in a food processor and blend until you have a stiff dough.
2. Divide the dough into 4. Squash each one down and sprinkle over the paprika. Using plenty of flour, roll the dough out as thin as you can. Cut into triangles.
3. Pour the oil into a large frying pan and heat. Try one of the chips to test the temperature of the fat; once the chip bubbles the fat is hot enough. Fry the chips in batches for about a minute each time. They should be lightly browned.
4. Drain on some kitchen paper and season with salt.
5. Serve with guacamole and dips.

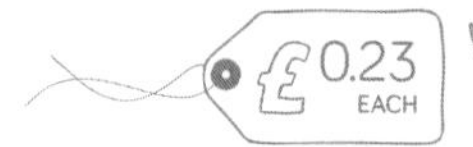

Parmesan Biscuits

Here we have served the Parmesan thins with some cold meats, pickles and veggie sticks to make a lovely snack meal.

100g **GF plain flour**

1 teaspoon **xanthan gum**

80g **butter**, measure using packet

80g grated **Parmesan**

½ teaspoon **dry mustard**

1 **egg**

1. Put the flour, xanthan gum, butter, Parmesan and mustard in a food processor and whizz until you have something resembling bread crumbs. Add the egg and pulse a few times until a dough is formed.
2. Tip out onto some cling film. Wrap and form a 5cm diameter 'sausage'. Place in the fridge for 30 minutes.
3. Preheat the oven to 180°C fan oven/200°C/gas 6. Grease a baking tray.
4. Cut the dough into 1cm slices and place on the baking tray. Bake in the oven for 12 minutes. The biscuits should be light, golden brown.

 We have got another recipe like this at noshbooks.com/cheesebiscuits

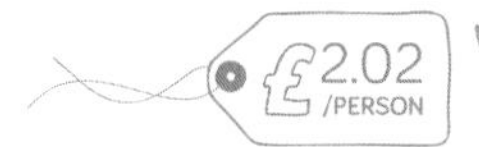

Cornbread and Chilli

Cornbread

280g **fine polenta**

90g **GF plain flour**

1 teaspoon **xanthan gum**

2 teaspoons **GF bicarbonate of soda**

pinch **salt**

150g grated **Cheddar cheese**

1 **egg**

150ml **milk**

425ml **buttermilk**

Chilli

2 tablespoons **olive oil**

1 **onion**

500g **minced beef**

2 cloves **garlic**, finely chopped

6 **tomatoes**, chopped

2 tablespoons **tomato purée**

1 **GF beef stock cube**

1 **fat red chilli**, chopped

1 mug **water**

1 tin **haricot beans**

2 tablespoons freshly chopped **coriander**

1 Preheat the oven to 190°C fan oven/210°C/gas 7. Grease a tray bake tin.

2 Mix together the dry ingredients for the cornbread. Mix together the wet ingredients and add together. Mix together, but don't overstir. Pour into the tin. Bake in the oven for 35–40 minutes. The bread should bounce back when lightly pressed and be golden brown on the top.

3 Meanwhile, make the chilli. Heat the oil in a large saucepan or wok, add the onions and fry until they begin to brown. Add the beef and fry until it is no longer pink.

4 Add the garlic, tomatoes, tomato purée, stock cube, chilli and water. Bring to the boil and simmer gently for 20 minutes.

5 Add the beans and coriander and heat through.

6 Serve with the cornbread and some salad.

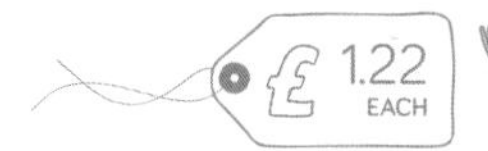

Cornish Pasties

1 tablespoon **olive oil**

1 **onion**, sliced

350g **beef stewing steak**

1 **potato**, cut into 2cm dice

$\frac{1}{3}$ **butternut squash**, cut into 2cm dice

1 **carrot**, peeled and cut into small dice

1 **sprig of rosemary**

3 mugs **water**

1 quantity of **basic shortcrust pastry**, see page 11

beaten **egg** to brush the pastry

1. Preheat the oven to 180°C fan oven/200°C/gas 6.
2. Heat the oil in a 'hob to oven' casserole dish. Fry the onions until they begin to soften.
3. Add the meat and fry until it is no longer pink on the outside. Season well with salt and pepper.
4. Add the potatoes, squash, carrot, rosemary and water and bring to the boil.
5. Place in the oven for $1\frac{3}{4}$ hours. Leave to cool.
6. Make the pastry. Roll out and cut into 4 circles, using a bowl approximately 15cm diameter as a guide.
7. Place $\frac{1}{4}$ of the cooled mixture in the centre, fold over the pastry and pinch together to form the pasty.
8. Place the pasties on a baking tray and brush with beaten egg. Bake in the oven for 20 minutes.

Layered Pancake Bake

Pancakes

3 **eggs**

180g **GF self-raising flour**

300ml **milk**

white Flora

Filling

200g **ham**, chopped

5 **spring onions,** chopped

1 tablespoon freshly chopped **basil**

1 tablespoon freshly chopped **parsley**

Sauce

100g grated **Gruyère cheese**

1 tablespoon **GF flour**

10g **butter**, measure using the packet

1/2 teaspoon **dried mustard**

1 mug/300ml **milk**

Topping

100g grated **Gruyère**

1 slice **GF bread**, made into breadcrumbs

1. Preheat the oven to 200°C fan oven/220°C/gas 7. Grease a large ovenproof dish.
2. Beat together the pancake ingredients. You should have a mixture with the consistency of double cream. Heat about a teaspoon of the Flora in a small frying pan. Add about 2 tablespoons of the pancake mixture and tip it around the pan to cover the bottom. Fry on each side until lightly browned. Make 5 pancakes and set to one side until needed.
3. Mix together the filling ingredients and season with salt and pepper.
4. Put the sauce ingredients in a small saucepan and gently bring to the boil, the sauce should be thickened. Season with salt and pepper.
5. Place one pancake on the bottom of the dish, add 1/4 of the filling and pour over 1/4 of the sauce. Place another pancake on top and add 1/4 of the filling and 1/4 of the sauce. Repeat this once more and add the last pancake on top. Pour over the rest of the sauce and top with the rest of the filling. Mix the breadcrumbs and cheese together for the topping and sprinkle over.
6. Place in the oven for 20 minutes.
7. Serve with some salad and salad dressing.

NOTE: We used a honey and lemon salad dressing. Juice of a lemon, 2 tablespoons extra virgin olive oil, 1 tablespoon honey + salt and pepper.

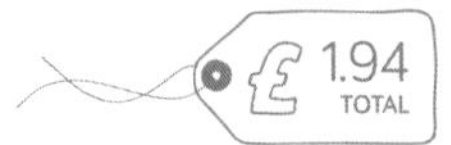

Brown Bread

Doves Farm brown bread flour has xanthan gum already added to it, so there is no need to add more.

- 100ml **warm water**
- 1½ tablespoons **sugar**
- 3 teaspoons **dried yeast**
- 1 teaspoon **white wine vinegar**
- 1 **egg** + 2 **egg whites**
- 65ml **olive oil**
- 2 tablespoons **honey**
- 2 tablespoons **soft brown sugar**
- 200ml **warm water**
- 400g **GF brown bread flour**
- ½ teaspoon **salt**

1. Preheat the oven to 170°C fan oven/190°C/gas 5. Grease a 3lb loaf tin.
2. Mix together the 100ml water with the sugar and yeast. Leave for about 10 minutes until it starts to puff up.
3. In a separate bowl, mix togther the white wine vinegar, the whole egg, olive oil, honey, sugar and the 200ml warm water.
4. Put the flour and salt in a large mixing bowl.
5. Beat the egg whites until stiff.
6. Once the yeast has started to work, mix everything with the flour.
7. The dough will be quite wet. Pour into the loaf tin and leave in a warm place for about 1 hour.
8. Place in the oven for 70 minutes. Take out of the tin and replace in the oven for a further 10 minutes. The loaf should sound 'hollow' when tapped on the bottom.

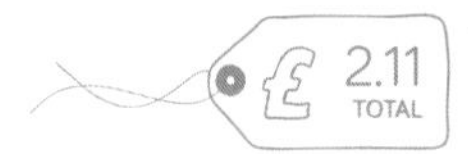

White Seeded Loaf

Doves Farm bread flour has xanthan gum already added to it, so there is no need to add more.

100ml warm **water**

1½ tablespoons **sugar**

3 teaspoons **dried yeast**

1 teaspoon **white wine vinegar**

1 **egg** + 2 **egg whites**

65ml **olive oil**

2 tablespoons **honey**

2 tablespoons **soft brown sugar**

180ml warm **water**

400g **GF white bread flour**

½ teaspoon **salt**

1 tablespoon **sesame seeds**

1 tablespoon **sunflower seeds**

1. Preheat the oven to 170°C fan oven/190°C/gas 5. Grease a 3lb loaf tin.
2. Mix together the 100ml water with the sugar and yeast. Leave for about 10 minutes until it starts to bubble up.
3. Mix togther the white wine vinegar, the whole egg, olive oil, honey, sugar and the 180ml warm water.
4. Put the flour, salt and seeds in a large mixing bowl.
5. Beat the egg whites in a separate bowl, until stiff.
6. Once the yeast has started to work, mix everything with the flour.
7. The dough will be quite wet. Pour into the loaf tin and leave in a warm place for about 1 hour.
8. Place in the oven for 70 minutes. Take out of the tin and replace in the oven for a further 10 minutes. The loaf should sound 'hollow' when tapped on the bottom.

Brioche

You can freeze the brioche in slices and use it to make a yummy bread and butter pudding, with raspberries, eggs, cream and little lemon zest.

325g **GF white bread flour**

1 teaspoon **xanthan gum**

1 teaspoon **salt**

3 teaspoons **dried yeast**

150g **butter**, measure using packet

75ml warm **water** + 125ml warm **milk**

2 **eggs**

3 tablespoons **runny honey**

1 Grease a loaf tin.

2 Put the flour, xanthan gum, salt, yeast and butter in a food mixer. Add the butter and mix on low speed, leaving the butter quite lumpy.

3 Mix together the warm milk, water, eggs and honey. Add to the bowl and mix on a low speed until everything is mixed together. The dough will be quite wet.

4 Put the dough in the loaf tin, spread out evenly and leave in a warm place for 1 hour.

5 Preheat the oven to 180°C fan oven/200°C/gas 6.

6 Place the loaf in the oven for 45 minutes.

7 Allow to cool a little. However, note that this brioche is best eaten whilst fresh.

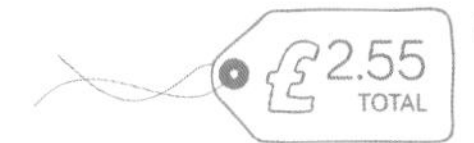

Almond Soda Bread

250g **GF white bread flour**

100g **almond flour**

2 teaspoons **xanthan gum**

3 teaspoons **GF bicarbonate of soda**

1 teaspoon **salt**

2 tablespoons **soft brown sugar**

300ml **buttermilk**

100ml **water**

1. Preheat the oven to 200°C fan oven/220°C/gas 7.
2. Combine the dry ingredients in a large bowl.
3. Mix the buttermilk and water together. Add to the dry ingredients and mix together. Don't over mix.
4. Turn out onto a floured surface and, with floured hands, shape into a loaf. The dough is quite wet.
5. Place on a lined baking tray and bake in the oven for 45–50 minutes. The loaf should be nicely browned and sound 'hollow' when tapped on the bottom.

Amazed at how easy making soda bread is? Then you'll want to try this other soda bread recipe at noshbooks.com/sodabread

Cheese and Onion Bread Rolls

50ml warm **water**

1 tablespoon **sugar**

1½ teaspoons **dried yeast**

200g **GF white bread flour**

1 teaspoon **GF baking powder**

1 teaspoon **xanthan gum**

½ teaspoon **salt**

1 **egg**, beaten

30ml **olive oil**

1 tablespoon **honey**

1 tablespoon **soft brown sugar**

90ml warm **water**

½ teaspoon **white wine vinegar**

Topping

½ **onion**, sliced

½ mug grated **Cheddar cheese**

1 dessertspoon **olive oil**

salt and **pepper**

1. Mix together the sugar and the 50ml water, sprinkle over the yeast and mix together. Leave in a warm place for 5–7 minutes or until the yeast begins to bubble.
2. Mix the flour, baking powder, xanthan gum and salt together in a large bowl.
3. Mix together the egg, olive oil, honey, sugar, the 90ml warm water and the white wine vinegar.
4. Once the yeast has begun to froth a little, add to the dry ingredients, along with the egg mix. Mix together, but do not beat. The dough will be quite soft.
5. Turn out onto a floured surface and cut into 4 pieces. Without kneading, form into bread buns. Place on a greased baking sheet and leave in a warm place for about 1 hour.
6. Preheat the oven to 170°C fan oven/190°C/gas 4.
7. Mix the topping ingredients together in a small bowl and spread over the top of the rolls.
8. Bake in the oven for 35 minutes. The tops will be nicely browned and the onions crisp.

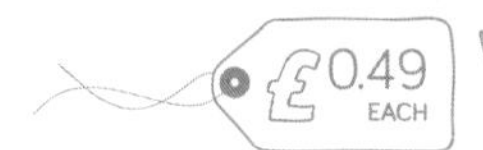

Stilton and Walnut Swirls

Dough

1 tablespoon **honey**

150ml **warm water**

1½ teaspoons **dried yeast**

200g **GF white bread flour**

1 teaspoon **GF baking powder**

1 teaspoon **xanthan gum**

½ teaspoon **salt**

1 **egg**

2 tablespoons **olive oil**

½ teaspoon **cider vinegar**

50g **walnuts**, chopped

100g **blue Stilton**

beaten egg for brushing

1. Put the honey, water and yeast in a small jug. Leave for about 5 minutes for the yeast to bubble and activate.
2. Mix together the flour, baking powder, xanthan gum and salt in a large bowl.
3. Mix together the egg, oil and cider vinegar. Add to the flour along with the yeast mixture. Mix together.
4. Turn out onto a floured sheet of cling film. Gently roll out the dough to approximately 30 x 20cm. Sprinkle with the cheese and walnuts. Use the cling film to help roll up the dough like a Swiss roll. Cut into slices and place on a greased baking sheet.
5. Leave in a warm place to prove for an hour.
6. Preheat the oven to 180°C fan oven/200°C/gas 6.
7. Brush the rolls with beaten egg and place in the oven for 30 minutes.

index

REGISTER

at noshbooks.com/gf to get
new gluten-free recipes
emailed to you
every month

Published by: Intrade (GB) Ltd
Contact: joymay@mac.com
ISBN: 978-0-9567464-9-8
Printed in China

1st Edition: July 2015. 2nd Print August 2016
Author: Joy May
Photography: Tim May at timmayphotography.co.uk
Design: Ben May at milkbottledesigns.co.uk
Proof-reading: Fran Maciver
Editor: Ron May

Some great brands have donated cooking gear for us to use. Thanks so much to:

KENWOOD

magimix